THE CASE FOR
PRIVATE ENTERPRISE

THE CASE FOR

PRIVATE ENTERPRISE

Editor: Cecil Turner

Foreword by

The Rt Hon Sir Keith Joseph Bt MP

Bachman & Turner Ltd
London

First published in 1979 by
Bachman & Turner Ltd
The Old Hop Exchange
1/3 Central Buildings
Southwark Street
London SE1

ISBN 0 85974 083 8
ISBN 0 85974 085 4

Typeset by Inforum Ltd, Portsmouth
Printed and bound in Great Britain by
Anchor Press Ltd, Tiptree, Essex

CONTENTS

To
Michael Marks
The founder of a
great enterprise

Foreword

IN DEFENCE OF FREE ENTERPRISE
by Sir Keith Joseph

Free enterprise has proved to be the greatest engine of material advance ever known; it has alleviated poverty, raised living standards, increased the quantity, quality and range of goods produced. From its profits have come patrons for the arts, charity and science, and the money to pay for public goods and services. Imperfect like all human institutions, it is nevertheless a great improver, its errors provide the spur to invention and adaptation.

The free enterprise order is also a great leveller: competition and innovation ensure that the luxury item which is enjoyed to-day by the affluent few quickly becomes the necessity of the masses. Indeed, although economists are wont to talk aridly about its "mechanisms", its "leads" and its "lags", it is essentially an organic, human process, constantly reflecting and responding to the myriad and changing needs of human beings, reconciling the interests of people as workers with the demands of the same people as consumers with greater sensitivity than anything dreamed up by the most ambitious and benevolent social engineer. Most importantly, free enterprise is a necessary condition of cultural and political liberty. For the decentralisation of ownership and decision-making which is the essence of the market order or free enterprise acts as a check on the accumulation of power by government and ensures that there is an infinitely wide range of potential patrons for every variety of political, cultural and economic diversity.

By contrast, socialist economic systems involving the allocation or strict control of resources by politicians or bureaucrats (or both) have signally failed. As Solzhenitsyn wrote in his letter to the Russian leaders, "Marx was mistaken when he forecast that the proletariat would be endlessly oppressed and would never achieve anything in a bourgeouis democracy: if only we could shower people with as much food, clothing and leisure as they have gained under capitalism". Even judged by the criteria of socialism, socialism has failed. There are many socialist nations but none in which freedom, equality and fraternity are more than hollow slogans.

Given the huge success of free enterprise and the momentous failures and tragedies of socialism, is it not remarkable that free enterprise should need to be defended — particularly from the champions of a system which has so conspicuously miscarried? In the case of free enterprise it might be said that nothing fails like success, while in the case of socialism, nothing succeeds like failure. The explanation of this paradox is surely that most social commentators have not been concerned with the outcome of either system. Certainly, they have been largely unimpressed by the economic successes of capitalism even when enjoying them — and the freedom which it buttresses — to the full. As Christopher Tame points out in his opening chapter, the basis of their objection to free enterprise is a *moral* one. Their view — wholly mistaken in my opinion — is that free enterprise is intrinsically evil because it is based on individual selfishness and greed. This belief has animated the writings not merely of socialist theoreticians but of historians, sociologists and economists — witness the way in which moral imperatives are implied in the writings of neo-Keynesian economists.

Lord Balogh, whose own writings on economics provide many examples of the way in which apparently objective scholarship reflects moral assumptions, recently provided evidence on how longstanding the moral hostility to free enterprise has been: "As a young student I was taught that economics is about welfare, the maximum possible satisfaction of human wants, *the lessening of inequality*". (Observer, 7th Jan. 1979). He has evidently been faithful to his mentors.

Inequality is not the only component of free enterprise to have been condemned on ethical grounds. Competition, private ownership and profits are also viewed with deep distaste by the egalitarian, usually without a prior understanding of their economic and social function. However, I do not wish to pre-empt what the authors of this volume have to say about the intellectual roots of the crusade against free enterprise, merely to touch on two aspects of the subject as it affects us to-day.

The first is to stress the extent to which business itself has been demoralised by the anti-business culture. Faced by the now hackneyed arguments about the immorality of this or that aspect of capitalism, the various spokesmen for free enterprise have frequently conceded part of their opponents' case rather in the manner of an accused man pleading guilty to a false charge in order to obtain clemency rather than risk the verdict going against him. Whatever the reasons, it is evident that many managers simply do not have confidence in or proper understanding of the economic order within which they work. This process of demoralisation has coincided with, and been enforced by, the bureaucratisation of industry and commerce by government and the extent to which economic and political pressures — themselves the result of misguided economic policy — have forced firms to seek subsidies and the other benefits available from the State (pleasing the government can be as important to survival as pleasing the consumer these days). It is not altogether surprising, therefore, that free enterprise — finding itself overwhelmed by red tape and bureaucracy, by legislation, regulation and price control, debilitated by historically high rates of inflation and taxation, intimidated by the monopoly power of belligerent trade unions and subject to a constant barrage of moral criticism — should lack the ability, and even the will, to defend itself.

I freely acknowledge that free enterprise has not been able to look to politicians to defend it. The Social Democrats in the Labour Party have paid lip service to the idea of a "mixed economy", without ever having spoken up for the part of the mix which was expected to finance all their schemes. Nor have they attended to the conditions in which it might do its beneficient work; on the contrary, they have destroyed them.

The lack of enthusiasm for free enterprise, displayed by the British Social Democrats, stems — I think — from the internal tensions within the Labour Party, from the mythology of the class war against the bosses, propagated over decades by the Labour Movement, from the link between the Labour Party and the trades unions and the intellectual temper of the Social Democrats themselves. A healthy and vigorous private sector requires adequate competition, unequal rewards, and profitability. At best, British Social Democrats have been lukewarm about such imperatives.

During the fifties, when British Social Democrats worked out their philosophy and programme, the emphasis was almost exclusively on redistribution, welfare and educational opportunities. Economic growth was taken for granted. It did not occur to most Social Democrats that the base of the welfare edifice which they were so busily constructing — the wealth- and job-creating and sustaining private sector — was increasingly threatened by the high levels of public spending which their ambitious schemes entailed. Their somewhat superior attitudes, derived mainly from Oxbridge and the Fabians, were certainly inimical to the needs of the entrepreneur whose rude energy, dynamism and flair provide the catalyst in

10

the free enterprise system, qualities which are apparently not congenial to Social Democratic sensibilities. One can certainly look in vain for a defence of entrepreneurship from a leading Social Democrat.

Nor has there been much awareness by Social Democrats of the threat posed to liberty by a top-heavy public sector directly employing nearly one-third of the workforce and consuming more than half the nation's resources.

The reaction of the Conservative Party to the ideological onslaught upon capitalism can be criticised on quite different grounds. There have been some stout defences of private enterprise, though few of them have met the arguments on moral grounds, and it has been the arguments from moral premises which have been the most telling. The reason for the Conservative Party's inability to mount a sufficiently robust defence of free enterprise is that the Conservative Party is not, by nature, a party of ideology.

There is no Tory dogma, no canon of immutable doctrine, least of all one based purely on economic laws; there is a Tory intellectual tradition, an accepted way of regarding the world. Confronted by the rise of a mass party, based very significantly on ideology, Conservatives went on behaving very much as they did in he 18th and 19th centuries. We did not recognise that a quite different response was required to that which is appropriate to opponents with whom there is no fundamental difference in values, no fundamental difference about the purpose of political activity.

We did not recognise that between pluralists and collectivists there can be no middle ground in ideas and no possibility of stealing one's opponents' electoral clothes without betraying the principles of a pluralistic society and our own intellectual tradition. Moreover, because of the comfortable backgrounds of many, though not all, Conservative MPs, there were considerable feelings of guilt which led the Party to accept and even champion measures which appeared beneficial but which proved destructive and which, perhaps, should not have been accepted at all.

With the benefit of hindsight, it is possible to conclude that the Tory tradition — with its emphasis on empiricism, scepticism, reluctance to changes based on dictat or blueprint, its unique conception of society as something organic — should have provided us with the knowledge and intellectual courage to protect and explain free enterprise more effectively that we did, and greater confidence to build a framework of laws and institutions within which free enterprise might flourish. It is plainly no use blaming the Conservative Party for having failed to behave like Friedmanites or Hayekians or latter-day Whigs, but I suspect that had we paid greater attention to our own tradition, we would have been better placed to resist the dubious attractions of social engineering, fine tuning, demand management, and all the other dirigiste measures which have so weakened enterprise and society as an organic entity.

The intellectual mood is now changing; one should no longer take for granted that any intelligent politically-interested person under 25 is a Socialist. Some may even be Conservatives. The Right in politics (for lack of a better term) is breeding its own intellectuals while tempting others away from socialism. There is now the beginnings of real defence of private enterprise — based on social, political and moral, as well as economic grounds. This book is part of the fight-back of those who still believe in an open, pluralistic and free society, of which free enterprise forms an indispensable and inseparable part.

EDITORIAL

Why do we need to draw attention to the merits of private enterprise when we are thought to be living in a largely private enterprise system? The answer is simple: its share of the national economy is diminishing.

Recently I heard a speech by Norris McWhirter, editor of the Guinness Book of Records and one of the founders of the National Association for Freedom (now The Freedom Association), in which he said that 29 people, out of every hundred working in this country, are working for the state or nationalised industries.

He added that the average person working here is occupied from January 1st until July 31 in providing direct and indirect taxes. Nearly 60% of the Gross National Product is being absorbed by taxation of one sort or another.

Within the pages of this modest book you will find the essential case for a market economy, namely that Private Enterprise enables the producer and the entrepreneur to be motivated by self-interest in supplying the consumer with the goods he wants at the most competitive prices.

This is why Michael Marks to whom this book is dedicated gave birth to that great enterprise affectionately called "Marks and Sparks" and why Freddie (now Sir Freddie) Laker undercut the world's great airlines and brought intercontinental travel within the reach of hundreds of thousands of people for the first time. Henry Ford created the T-type Ford for the millions just as Morris, once upon a long time ago, introduced the £100 car.

Among the millions of people who inhabit these

islands, there are thousands of "self-starters", people able to initiate, create, invent, organise, innovate. The Private Enterprise system gives them the opportunity to offer their goods or services to their prospective customers. Many fail but many more succeed. Without their efforts much that we take for granted would disappear. Variety would give way to uniformity, interest to monotony, plenty would be replaced by scarcity and numerous aspects of freedom would concede victory to dictatorship.

The distinguished writers in this symposium tell us why and how and to them I am grateful for the valuable contributions they have made.

THE CASE FOR
PRIVATE ENTERPRISE

Chris R Tame is a graduate of the University of Hull. Formerly on the staff of the Institute of Economic Affairs he was until recently the Head of the Research Department of the National Association for Freedom. He is now running The Alternative Bookshop, in Floral Street, Covent Garden which specialises in books on all aspects of individual liberty and the free market. He has been Co-Editor of *Counterattack*, the magazine of the Association of Self-Employed People, and is also Secretary of the Adam Smith Club and a member of the Executive of the Libertarian Alliance.

He is the author of numerous articles in both scholarly and political journals, including:

"Change and Pseudo-Change in Sociology", *Jewish Journal of Sociology,* June 1977.

"Man, Concepts and Society" and (with M. Brady) "A Note on Lionel Robbins", in *Wertfrei*, Spring 1974.

"The Revolution of Reason: Peter Gay, the Enlightenment and the Ambiguities of Classical Liberalism", *Journal of Libertarian Studies*, Summer 1977.

"Max Stirner in Context: The Profanization of Hegelianism and the Genesis of Marx's Historical Materialism", *Minus One*, No. 32, 1973.

"Against the New Mercantilism: The Relevance of Adam Smith", *Il Politico* (forthcoming).

Other articles by him have appeared in *Libertarian Forum, New Libertarian Notes, Libertarian Connection, The Match!, The New Banner, Counterattack,* and *The Guerilla Capitalist*, and he is a frequent contributor to *The Free Nation*. He is also the author of *The Politics of Whim: A Critique of the Situationist — Marxist Anthology 'Leaving the Twentieth Century'* and Editor of two forthcoming works, *For Adam Smith: New Essays in Classical Liberal Thought* and *A Bibliography of Freedom*.

1

THE MORAL CASE FOR PRIVATE ENTERPRISE
by Chris R. Tame

> "The New Intellectuals must fight for capitalism, not as a 'practical' issue, not as an economic issue, but, with the most righteous pride, as a *moral* issue. That is what capitalism deserves, and nothing less will save it". Ayn Rand, *For the New Intellectual.*

To examine the nature of the socialist tradition and the socialist case against private enterprise and the free market is a daunting task. Under its common banner we find many and diverse themes and motivations. And yet, amidst the diversity we can distinguish one common, and, I would argue, predominant theme — that of the *moral* evil of private ownership, the profit motive, and "selfish" private enterprise.

We thus find that socialists and Marxists are rarely content to rest their case against capitalism on a simple "exploitation" argument: that the individual is being robbed of his rightful property, and that the masses are unjustly being prevented from obtaining the good things in life. This approach would be — is — an individualistic moral position. Its premises are that the individual is the rightful owner of his self and his property, should profit from it (be the rightful beneficiary of his own actions), and is rightfully concerned with obtaining material goods and the pleasures of the world. (1) However, what we find in countless thinkers and writers is a moral attack on private enterprise as constituting individualism and selfishness. The individual, it is held, should serve others, "society" or some greater collective good, rather than be concerned with his own interest.

The Socialist Moral Tradition

We can trace this socialist moral tradition through virtually the whole range of socialist thinkers (and "precursors" of socialism). (2) It runs clearly through the earliest of "utopian" socialists like Mably and Morelly, Babeuf and Buonarotti, through Fourier to the more "modern" and "scientific" pre-Marxians like the Saint-Simonians and Auguste Comte. It was the latter who actually coined the term "altruism" to denote the placing of others and their interests before self, and sought the "scientific" and total subjugation of the individual to the collective. The tradition continued through the collectivist nationalists like Mazzini, who were equally vehement in their denunciation of the "fatal crime of egotism". And in the German philosopher Fichte the hatred of "selfishness" becomes, as J. L. Talmon points out, a "yearning for self-surrender" and "the utter annihilation of the individual".(3)

The relatively recent scholarly concentration on Marx's early writings, particularly the Paris Manuscripts and the *Grundrisse*, clearly demonstrates, however, the ethical motivation and normative content which later tended to be obscured by the structure of "scientific socialism" and historical materialism.(4) In the early Marx we are almost swamped by the incessant denunciation of the "egoism of trade", of man as "private individual" and "fractional being" in "civil society". Thus Marx rejected contemptuously the "rights of man" as (quite correctly, of course), the rights of "egoistic man". In his notorious essay "On the Jewish Question" the *"anti-*

social element" of Judaism — "*practical* need, *self-inter-est*" — was taken as symbolic of capitalism in general. This anti-social selfishness, in Marx's view, thus "sever(s) all man's species-ties, substitute(s) egoism and selfish need for those ties, and dissolve(s) the human world into a world of atomistic, mutually hostile individuals".(5) The ideal for Marx was man as "species being", in a state of collectivist, non-egoistic consciousness in which even his senses would be "emancipated" and "truly human" when "need or satisfaction have ... lost their *egoistic* nature".(6)

The same anti-egoism was as vehement in German National Socialism (Nazism), the manifesto of the National Socialist Workers Party of Germany proclaiming that "The activities of the individual may not clash with the interests of the whole, but must proceed within the frame of the community and be for the general good ... THE COMMON INTEREST BEFORE SELF".(7) Hitler himself was, in *Mein Kampf*, as vigorous as Marx in his denunciation of "greed and materialism", and called for "not material selfishness, but readiness for sacrifice and joy in renunciation".(8) Likewise, Italian fascism, as enunciated by Benito Mussolini was fundamentally concerned with "suppressing the instinct for a life enclosed within the brief round of pleasure in order to restore within duty a higher life free from the limits of time and space: a life in which the individual, through the denial of himself, through the sacrifice of his own private interests, through death itself, realises that completely spiritual existence in which his value as a man lies".(9)

In Britain, our own distinctively less dramatic and more boring variety of socialism manifest in Fabianism was equally hostile to "selfishness" and materialism. For Sydney Webb "the perfect and fitting development of each individual is not necessarily the utmost and highest cultivation of his own personality, but the filling, in the

19

best possible way, of his humble function in the great social machine".(10) Indeed, in Beatrice Webb that hostility to individualism and egoism reaches a pathological extreme, calling for "the sacrifice of individual life and happiness ... the greatest of human characteristics, the power of self-sacrifice in the individual for the good of the community".(11) Fascinated by the Buddhist state of Nirvanic self-obliteration she declared that "to me, human personality as I know it — myself and others — is a tragedy ... I long to rid myself of my personality".(12)

At the present time the socialist moral consensus is virtually unchallenged. The works of the late Richard Titmus, with their tediously expounded message of the "supreme ethic of service rather than the mundane aim of profit"(13), provide the substance of countless University degrees in social policy and administration. And the constant refrain of the Labour "Left" is against the "selfish, avaricious, materialistic philosophy of capitalism which says every man for himself" (as Joan Maynard MP put it).(14)

The Moral Abdication of the Liberal Tradition

Tragically, however, the liberal defenders of private enterprise and capitalism have almost universally abdicated from the tasks of replying to the socialist moral critique. Their arguments have largely centered on the *economic* superiority of capitalism — its ability to "deliver the goods" — while, at best, ignoring moral issues, or, at worst, even conceding the socialists' premises.

Even Adam Smith, the very founder of both free market economics and the liberal political tradition, could declare, in *The Theory of Moral Sentiments*, that "man was made to promote ... the happiness of all".(15) As one Smith scholar has observed, "It was not to serve the selfish benefit of the individual that he should be given

20

his head . . . the belief that Smith was primarily an individualist . . . is the very reverse of the truth. For him . . . the interests of society were the end".(16)

And thus, even at the height of their intellectual predominance, liberals failed to challenge the moral case of their rising socialist opponents. In that bastion of militant liberalism, the *Cobden Club Essays*, we find Joseph Gostick attempting to reply to socialism in the following manner: "The error of communistic theories", he wrote, "is that they seek to gain, by a change of formal institutions, results that, if ever attainable, can be reached only by a long and severe education of human nature. When these results are obtained, when the three higher principles — sympathy, benevolence, and self-sacrifice — have gained a sure and final predominance over the four lower — egotism, acquisition, emulation, and legal strife — *then* communistic theories, requiring the industrious to work for the idle, and the able to sacrifice themselves for the incapable may be found possible, but at that time we shall want neither these nor any other theories, we shall be simply translated into Paradise".(17)

An impractical, but nevertheless noble ideal! Such was the general liberal view of socialism. William Lecky lauded the "nobler motives", the "conception of the purely disinterested . . . the noblest thing we possess, the celestial spark that is within us". The "moral elevation of an age" he judged by the intensity of the spirit of self sacrifice. And the "love of wealth", although admittedly "beneficial" in its consequences, is "far less noble" and "contract(s) and indurat(es) the character".(18) Similarly, Henry Sidgwick the liberal economist and political philosopher, contrasted unfavourably the so-called "selfish struggle of individuals" with the "mutual service and general diffusion of public spirit".(19) Although "admittedly advantageous to production" it was quite clear that Sidgwick abhorred what he saw as "the anti-social temper and attitude of mind, produced by the continual

21

struggle of competition". This "moral aversion to private enterprise", Sidgwick admitted, was an important motivation "in the impulses that lead thoughtful persons to embrace some form of socialism". Even for those — like himself — who were not socialists, Sidgwick continued, and who "(regard) the stimulus and direction of energy given by the existing individualistic system as quite indispensable to human society as yet present constituted, yet feel the moral need of some means of developing in the members of a modern industrial community a fuller consciousness of their industrial work as a social function, only rightly performed when done with a cordial regard to the welfare of the whole society. . .".(20)

It would not be going too far to say that liberalism as an ideology committed suicide. Who after all — and especially among young people — will crusade for a movement and a way of life which declares itself morally flawed, "practical" but basically immoral?

And yet the few contemporary alleged defenders of private enterprise and capitalism are still plowing the same barren furrow. Peregrine Worsthorne actually *praises* capitalism for being "such a uniquely modest economic system in terms of moral pretensions" and claims that "the capitalist system is a non-moral or amoral way of organising and distributing wealth".(21) Edward Norman, who, marginally more ambitious, declares that "the morality of capitalism is about the morality of choice" does not get to grip with the fundamental issues. And, similarly, he labels the moral outlook of capitalism as, contrary to "Humanism", an unoptimistic one which regards men as "inherently defective".(22) Even amidst the ranks of today's most gifted liberal scholars we find little more than demolition of the *economic* idiocies of socialism(23), or, in Hayek's essay "The Moral Element in Free Enterprise"(24), a discussion of generally secondary matters. Yeats' lines sum up, probably better than any others the bleak situation resulting from liberalism's failure — one where

"The best lack all conviction while the worst
Are full of passionate intensity".

The Virtue of "Selfishness": The Moral Case for Private Enterprise

As paradoxical as it might seem then, the American liberal Rose Wilder Lane was fundamentally correct when she declared that the classical liberals "have not grasped (the) basic individualistic principle at all . . . (their) basic *assumption* is communist".

But if the liberals abdicated from the task of a vigorous moral defence of capitalism we can at least thank our enemies for their frank and correct identification of the central issues. For it is precisely the "selfishness" of private enterprise that constitutes its moral virtue, its moral *glory*. Put aside for the moment the immense moral stigma — and intimidation — so successfully injected into the term "selfishness" by generations of collectivist propagandists, and consider the *real* meaning of the moral dichotomy between socialism and capitalism. Capitalism holds that the individual possesses the right to exist for his own sake, the right to life, liberty and property. Socialism quite clearly does not, but rather holds the view that individuals are duty bound to sacrifice their life, liberty and property for the good of some collective, whether "the people", "the nation", "the race", "the fatherland" or whatever, depending upon the particular brand of socialism. Marx was quite right, then, in declaring the capitalist liberal concept of individual rights as "egoistic rights". Either the individual exists as an entity of value, for his own sake, as an end in himself and not a means to the ends of others, or he exists as a creature bound to work for the sake of others. There is a word for those commanded to exist and labour for the sake of others — *slaves*. The morality of socialism is the morality of slavery.

The barbarities of the countless "noble" socialist experiments, the atrocities of Hitler, Lenin, Stalin, or the Cambodian communists, are not, then, simply historical "accidents"; they are the logical, *inevitable* products of altruist morality, the creed of "unselfishness". As the American philosopher Ayn Rand has put it: "If service and self-sacrifice are a moral ideal, and if the 'selfishness' of human nature prevents men from leaping into sacrificial furnaces, there is no reason ... why a dictator should not push them in at the point of bayonets — for their own good, or the good of humanity, or the good of posterity, or the good of the latest bureaucrat's latest five year plan. There is no reason that (socialists) can name to oppose *any* atrocity. The value of a man's life? His right to exist? His right to pursue his own happiness? These are concepts that belong to individualism and capitalism — to the antithesis of altruist morality".(25)

Of course, socialists will try to drag the inevitable "red" herrings across the path of this argument. The immediate image they manage to link to the term selfishness is one of brutal rapacity, dishonesty, lack of concern for the rights of others etc. In fact, since the term means literally concern for one's self interest, their reaction is really a rather telling confession of the view of what is in their interest, and of their inability to conceive of a society in which non-sacrificial, non-violent, non-compulsory co-operation and co-existence is possible between individuals. It is not, of course, in the individual's interest, either physically or psychologically, to live in such an unhuman (and inhumane) manner. The glory of capitalism is that it is precisely the system — as economic analysis and historical experience have repeatedly demonstrated — in which all individuals profit and prosper by "serving" each other in the market, where their selfish seeking of profit guides them, as if by an "invisible hand" as Adam Smith so notably put it, to provide each other with goods and services.

The other red herring inevitably to be met is, of course, of the "you mean you wouldn't help an abandoned baby found in the streets" sort. It is an argument which equates any benevolence, good will or assistance to others with self-sacrifice and altruism. In fact, helping others rests precisely upon the individualist, "selfish" premise, that human beings are values and ends in themselves. It is altruism which in fact devalues individual lives and holds them as objects of sacrifice for others or some alleged "greater good".

It is a monument to the immense and unchallenged authority built up by the altruist morality that hardly any-one penetrates the almost idiotic mystifications, "false consciousness", and illogicalities inherent in it. For exam-ple, if it is good to work for the sake of others, and not for personal private profit, one is actually left in a sort of cir-cular position where 'A' works for 'B' who works for 'C' and so on *ad infinitum.* But why should 'B' enjoy the good provided by 'A' when he is forbidden to enjoy the same good if he provides it for himself (but in turn has to provide it for 'C')? In fact, it seems clear from their words that many socialists seem to find material goods wicked in themselves. Their "morality" is one of austerity, asceti-cism, renunciation and poverty. It provides a fitting ideo-logy for the reality of life under socialist planning.

Moreover, the socialist "morality" of altruism provides a tremendously useful ideological disguise for all forms of tyranny. For if sacrifice is to be its watch-word and policy, then there has to be someone both dic-tating and *collecting* the sacrifice. And since "society", "the public interest", "the state", etc. do not exist as con-crete entities, it will be their self-appointed spokesmen dictating who will be doing the sacrificing and who will be receiving the benefits.

It is impossible of course, in this brief essay to outline

fully the philosophy of "ethical egoism", and its epistemological roots and validation, which underlies the private enterprise system. Fortunately there is now a growing number of intellectuals and academics who, following the seminal work of the American philosopher and novelist Ayn Rand, have recognised the moral code implicit in capitalism and are systematically expounding and elaborating it.(26) For the first time for centuries the "virtue of selfishness" and capitalism are being recognised and a *moral* battle is being fought for them. With its banner at last unfurled with moral pride and idealism, capitalism is now attracting the commitment and support of young people who recognise the wisdom of Ayn Rand's words:

> "The world crisis of today is a *moral* crisis — and nothing less than a moral revolution can resolve it . . . let those who care about the future, those willing to crusade for a perfect society, realise that the new *radicals* are the fighters for capitalism . . . to win requires your total dedication and a total break with the world of your past, with the doctrine that man is a sacrificial animal who exists for the pleasure of others. Fight for the value of your person . . . fight with the radiant certainty and absolute rectitude of knowing that yours is the Morality of Life and that yours is the battle for any achievement, any value, any grandeur, any goodness, and any joy that has ever existed on this earth"(27).

NOTES
(The numbers refer to the text)

(1) This is particularly apparent in the English pre-Marxian exponent of exploitation theory, Thomas Hodgskin. See Alexander Gray's account in *The Socialist Tradition*, Longmans, Green and Co., London, Second Imp., 1947, pp. 277-288. Gray, largely a critic of socialism, ironically finds Hodgskin's position tending to "a somewhat revolting and selfish individualism"! (p. 282).

(2) Of course, there are exceptions to this generally anti-egoist, anti-individualist stream of socialism. See, for example, Aaron Noland, "Individualism in Jean Jaures' Socialist Thought", *Journal of the History of Ideas*, Vol. XXII, No. 1, Jan-March 1961. Oscar Wilde's essay, "The Soul of Man under Socialism", in *Intentions and Other Writings*, Doubleday, Garden City, N.Y., n.d., also defends socialism in egoistic terms, as a means of sustaining a "new individualism". The British Bakuninite-Marxist Guy Aldred similarly did not attack self interest, but proclaimed "selfishness ... at the root of all social and industrial development", *Studies in Communism*, The Strickland Press, Glasgow, 1940, p 9. He sought a "sound and sane collectivism" for the sake and in terms of, a "practical individualism". See my own essay, "Guy Aldred", *The Match!*, Vol. 6, No. 1, Jan. 1975, for a further treatment. There were also some "Nietzschean" Marxists among the Russian Bolsheviks, of whom Stanislav Volski would appear to be the most genuine individualist. See George L. Kline, "'Nietzschean Marxists' in Russia", in F. J. Adelman, ed., *Demythologizing Marxism*, Boston College, Chestnut Hill, 1969. Such cases of individualist oriented socialists should not be confused, however, with various "dialectical" exponents of "new" and "higher" alleged individualisms, who seek to blot out real distinctions in conceptual fuzziness. For example, Steven Lukes, *Individualism*, Basil Blackwell, Oxford, 1978, and Ellen M. Wood, *The Mind and Politics: An Approach to the Meaning of Liberal and Socialist Individualism*, University of California Press, 1972.

(3) Alexander Gray, *op cit*; Emile Durkheim, *Socialism and Saint Simon*, Routledge, London, 1959; J. L. Talmon, *Political Messianism: The Romantic Phase*, Secker and Warburg, 1960, p 195.

(4) See especially Eugene Kamenka, *The Ethical Foundations of Marxism*, Routledge, London, 1962 and *Marxism and Ethics*, Macmillan, London, 1969. As Kamenka points out in the latter work: "As Marx the philosopher became somewhat submerged beneath Marx the social scientist (the) ethical impulse was to some extent hidden from view by accretions from other sources — by the materialist critique of moralities, by Darwinian strains, by a concentration on material needs that bore a superficial resemblance to utilitarianism", p 3.

(5) "On the Jewish Question", in L. D. Easton and K. H. Guddat (eds), *Writings on the Young Marx on Philosophy and Society*, Doubleday, Garden City, N.Y., 1967, pp 237, 240, 243, 247.

(6) "Private Property and Communism", *Ibid*, p 308.

(7) Quoted in Eugene Weber, *Varieties of Fascism: Doctrines of Revolution in the Twentieth Century*, D. Van Nostrand, N.Y.,

1964, p 154.

(8) Adolf Hitler, *My Struggle*, Hurst and Blackett, London, 1937, pp 118, 167.

(9) Benito Mussolini, "The Doctrine of Fascism", in Michael Oakeshott, *The Social and Political Doctrines of Contemporary Europe*, Basis Books, London, 1940, p 164.

(10) Alexander Gray, *The Socialist Tradition, op cit*, p 397.

(11) Quoted in Shirley Letwin, *The Pursuit of Certainty*, Cambridge University Press, 1965, pp 360, 351.

(12) *Ibid*, p 350.

(13) D. A. Reisman, *Richard Titmus: Welfare and Society*, Heinemann Educational Books, London, 1977, p 124.

(14) *The Star*, November 26, 1975.

(15) Quoted, p 219, in T. D. Cambell, *Adam Smith's Science of Morals*, Allen and Unwin, London, 1971.

(16) A. L. Macfie, *The Individual in Society: Papers on Adam Smith*, Allen and Unwin, London, 1967, p 54.

(17) Joseph Gostick, "Trade-Unions, and the Relations of Capital and Labour", in Emile de Laveleye et al. *Cobden Club Essays*, 2nd Series, 1871-2, Cassell, Petter and Galpin, London, 1872, pp 391-392.

(18) William Leckey, *History of the Rise and Influence of the Spirit of Rationalism in Europe*, Watts, London, 1910, Vol. 2, pp 135, 81, 105.

(19) Henry Sidgwick, *The Elements of Politics*, 3rd edn., Macmillan, London, 1908, p 158.

(20) *Ibid*, p 589. Another illuminating example of the liberal acquiescence before the moral attack was in one writer's attempted reply to George Bernard Shaw in the 1920's: "Now it is true", wrote Lillian Le Mesurier, "and may be gladly acknowledged that there are people, saints and heroes whose stimulus and strong motive is not one of personal advantage but a spiritual motive: it is the service of God and their neighbour. Let us be thankful for them: It is they who lead the race up towards the stars. . . . We know with shame that we cannot walk with them upon the heights and breathe the rare air which they breathe, being as yet on a lower and more material plane. . . . To work for the sake of profit is not so noble an aim as to work for the sake of service: it is not the highest principle, but — it answers! It is as vain to try and run industry on principles which are far ahead of the common spiritual level. . . . Yet Socialists persist in talking as if human nature were entirely different to what it manifestly is". Lillian Le Mesurier, *The Socialist Woman's Guide to Intelligence: A Reply to Mr. Shaw*, Ernest Benn, London, 1929, pp 69-70.

(21) Peregrine Worsthorne, "Religion and the Fall of Capitalism", *The Sunday Telegraph*, 2nd November, 1975.

(22) "Capitalism as a Moral Defence Against the State", *The Daily Telegraph*, 21st March, 1978.

(23) For example, Yale Brozen, "A Corporate Rebuttal to: 'Profit is Inherently Unethical'", in Yale Brozen, et al. *Corporate Responsibility: The Viability of Capitalism in an Era of Militant Demands*, Rockford College Institute, Rockford, Illinois, 1978.

(24) In Friedrich Hayek, *Studies in Philosophy, Politics and Economics*, Simon and Schuster, New York, 1969. H. B. Acton's *The Morals of Markets: An Ethical Exploration*, Longmans, London, 1971, also largely misses the central ethical issues.

(25) Ayn Rand, *Faith and Force: The Destroyers of the Modern World*, The Objectivist, New York, 1960, p 11.

(26) See particularly, Ayn Rand, *For the New Intellectual*, New American Library, New York, 1961; *The Virtue of Selfishness: A New Concept of Egoism*, New American Library, New York, 1964; *Capitalism: The Unknown Ideal*, New American Library, New York, 1967. Miss Rand's two major novels, *The Fountainhead*, Panther Books, London, 1961, and *Atlas Shrugged*, New American Library, New York, 1957, are magnificent portrayals of her philosophy. Professor John Hospers deals with her approach in his best-selling texts, *An Introduction to Philosophical Analysis*, Routledge, London, rev. edn., 1967, and *Readings in Introductory Philosophical Analysis*, Routledge, London, 1969. Tibor Machan's *Human Rights and Human Liberties*, Nelson Hall, Chicago, 1975, also provides a clear statement. Dr. Nathaniel Branden has explored the psychological aspects and importance of ethical egoism in a number of works, including: *The Psychology of Self-Esteem*, Bantam Books, New York, 1971; *Breaking Free*, Bantam Books, New York, 1972; "Psychotherapy and the Objectivist Ethics", in B.A. Ard, Jr., ed., *Counselling and Psychotherapy: Classics in Theories and Issues*, Science and Behaviour Books, Palo Alto, California, 1966. It should also be pointed out that this ethical egoist position is very much a more systematic extension of the now almost totally neglected Aristotelian-Thomistic tradition of philosophy with its concern for, as one exponent puts it "the practical business of living intelligently". See Henry B. Veatch, *Aristotle: A Contemporary Appreciation*, Indiana University Press, Bloomington, 1974; *Rational Man: A Modern Interpretation of Aristotelian Ethics*, Indiana University Press, Bloomington, 1962.

(27) *For The New Intellectual*, New American Library, New York, 1961, pp 54, 192.

Henry Stanley Ferns was born in Canada and educated there and at Trinity College, Cambridge. From 1940-45, he was a member of the secretarial staff of the Prime Minister of Canada and the Canadian Department of External Affairs. Since 1950 he has taught in the University of Birmingham, where he is Professor of Political Science. He had a part in the foundation of Britain's only institution of higher education which is independent of government, the University College at Buckingham, of which he is an honorary fellow. He has written (with B. Ostry) *The Age of Mackenzie King* (London, 1955; Toronto, 1976); *Britain and Argentina in the Nineteenth Century* (Oxford, 1960; Buenos Aires, 1967; New York, 1976); *Argentina* (London, 1969); *Towards an Independent University* (London, 1969); *National Economic Histories: The Argentine Republic* (Newton Abbot, 1973); *The Disease of Government* (London, 1978).

2

PROPERTY, SELF-INTEREST AND COMPETITION
by H. S. Ferns

It is an incontrovertible fact that free enterprise communities produce more goods and services and distribute them better than communities where politicians and/or soldiers control the economy. The contrast in terms of goods and services consumed by the average citizen or by all of them between the U.S.A. and the U.S.S.R. between Mexico and Cuba, between West Germany and East Germany is so obvious and so striking that in any debate about the comparative merits of free enterprise market systems and government controlled and planned economies, one would suppose that the appeal to experience would be so conclusive that no one could say anything in favour of socialism, bureaucracy, communism and planning.

But this is not the case. Far too often the supporters of free enterprise find themselves overwhelmed by massive moral generalisations about democracy, social justice, humanitarianism, social harmony, love, equality, etc., etc., which are all in some way assumed to be both goals and the consequences of planning, state control, socialism and communism. The free enterprisers can point to the facts, but the socialists, communists and nationalisers too often have the best rhetoric and the most appealing arguments. Why?

The supporter of free enterprise is handicapped by the

absence of a simple, morally based analysis of free enterprise. The discussion of free enterprise and market economies is largely in the hands of academic economists and technical specialists in analysis and in advertising whose underlying mental training has been based on the social sciences. Economics and the social sciences in general have become so technical and specialized that their underlying moral and intellectual assumptions have ceased to be comprehensible and have often been forgotten. The arguments for free enterprise have become hard to present for want of the kind of simplicity and clarity which, for example, Adam Smith was able to employ in exposing the absurdities of the mercantilist controls exercised by the state in the eighteenth century.

In order to achieve some simplicity, clarity and moral appeal in the discussion of free enterprise and the market economy, it is necessary to understand three concepts: the concept of property; of self-interest and of competition. In the vocabulary of the socialists, the communists and the bureaucratic elite, property, self-interest and competition are dirty words, and it is a fact, sad but true, that the vocabulary of the left is now the dominant vocabulary in Britain: in the schools and institutions of higher education; in the media, in politics and in the churches. Property, self-interest and competition have become taboo subjects much as the public discussion of anything to do with sex was taboo in Victorian society.

The concept of property supposes the right of ownership, i.e. the right of absolute control: to consume, to enjoy, to use, not to use, to lend and to exchange for property belonging to others. But ownership of what? The most fundamental piece of property a man or woman can have is his or her own person with that person's capacity to work, i.e. to create material goods or perform services for himself or herself or for others. Work is the origin of all property and is the most fundamental of all human activities. One who does not own his or her own person is neither free nor even fully human. That is why it has been necessary to abolish slavery, which is the total ownership of persons by other persons, and feudal social relations, which involves the partial ownership of persons by other persons, in order to create a free enterprise, market economy.

If one's own person is one's own property this means that one has the right of disposal of the goods or services which one produces or renders. This right of disposal implies a right to use or to exchange in accordance with one's self-interest. One can, for example, exchange one's labour (i.e. the activity of providing a good or a service) for goods or services which one consumes immediately or in a short span of time, or one can exchange it (or part of it) for a promise of goods and services at some future time. Exchanging a present asset for a future asset supposes that in society there are some who do not need all their assets for their immediate needs and some who have needs in excess of their present capacity to produce goods and services. By exchanging present assets for promises to provide assets in the future, men and women are able to co-operate with one another, to develop a division of labour among themselves, and to increase the productivity of their individual labour, their co-operative activity and the use of tools of greater and greater complexity and sophistication.

Any system of exchange supposes the exchange of goods and services for goods and services. These exchanges are governed by self-interest, i.e. by the propensity to maximise one's own acquisition of goods and services. Both reason and experience demonstrate, however, that self-interest must be defined and limited. If this is not done there exists the possibility that individuals will seek to effect exchanges of nothing for something. In terms of pure self-interest this is the best exchange one can make. Such exchanges of nothing for something are made by force or by fraud or by both.

In order that the practice of exchanging property (i.e. the fruits of labour) for other property can be established as a means of social co-operation, it is therefore necessary to develop rules or customs which exclude the use of violence and fraud, and insure that goods and services are exchanged for goods and services.

The concept of self-interest therefore requires some definition. As a concept it is open ended, but only on the assumption that the parties to an exchange have both rights *and* duties: the right to offer a good or a service and the duty to offer one which *can be* refused.

Self-interest is a deeply rooted characteristic of human beings and, indeed, of all animals, but both in its intensity and its modes of expression, self-interest is extremely variable: from the totally selfish materialist to the saint, totally divested of material and emotional desires, whose sole interest is union with God. How one defines one's self-interest and how one seeks to achieve it is itself an aspect of self-interest.

Both reason and experience suggest that the very great variety of self-interest in individuals and collections of individuals precludes the possibility, except by chance, of a harmony or parallelism of interests. It is furthermore a matter of observation that the pursuit of self-interest can be destructive of individuals or society or both. It is, therefore, a problem for men and women generally to discover some method of containing and controlling a force so universal and so actually or potentially destructive.

Of all the solutions of this problem of self-interest, the most productive of harmony and co-operation is the set of social arrangements we call a laisser-faire, market economy.

In the first place a market economy involves the acknowledgement of self-interest as an important and indeed central psychic force in individuals. A market economy avoids the delusive artifice of concealing self-interest in the rhetoric of benevolence, which is the observed practice of bureaucratic empire builders, politicians and reformers of various kinds.

In the second place a market economy tends to focus self-interest on the necessary and predominantly healthy activity of exchanging goods and services for goods and services and to divert it from political, intellectual and religious goals, which are not susceptible to agreed definition and have a protean capacity to generate antagonism and even destruction. Thinking and feeling about religion, philosophy, politics and art are inevitable and indispensable human activities, but they are necessarily private, personal activities whose character is transformed and then destroyed if they "go public" and are made into rallying cries of contending interests. The production and exchange of goods and services on the other hand, are both private and, through the agency of market arrangements, public activities, which, because they are both necessary and specific, have only a limited power to produce irreconcilable differences out of which spring wars and social disasters.

In the third place, a market economy breaks down and defines self-interest so that only individuals or small aggregations of individuals — associations, corporations, trade unions and so on — confront one another. Confrontation of self-interested parties in a market supposes an outcome involving some kind of shared benefits from a transaction, and whatever the shared benefits may be they are unlikely to involve the total lives and all the interests of the parties to the transaction. It is quite possible in a market economy for self-interested parties confronting one another in determining the price of a commodity or the wages to be paid for a service to be otherwise friends and neighbours and fellow citizens. Even their confrontation in the market is limited and is but a stage in reaching an agreement to co-operate: to pay x pounds for a ton of copper or to pay y pounds an hour for labour or z pounds for a piece of technical advice. In short, a market decentralises self-interest and prevents it from aggregating and building up to the point of explosion — as collective self-interest does in political or religious confrontations. The history of Europe and of the world during most of the nineteenth century was rather peaceful compared with its history in the eighteenth and the twentieth centuries. Perhaps the growth of market economies had something to do with this difference, and their decline in importance as central agencies of social organisation something to do with the war and rumours of wars so much present for at least three-quarters of this century.

The third concept central to any system of free enterprise is competition. This concept embraces the notion of free participation in the activity of producing goods and/or services and the exchanging of the same. A market economy is a social mechanism for making decisions about prices, i.e. the determination in terms of money of the rate at which goods and services exchange for one another. No individual or corporation can say what a price is or should be. Only the participants in a market can say what a price is or should be, although many wish they could. The participants in a market can say what a price is by stating what amount of assets each is willing to give up to acquire the goods or services on offer. The participant who makes the largest offer accepted by buyers determines the price of the good or service on offer. This price is what the seller must accept and the buyer pay. This price will determine the decisions of sellers about whether they wish or are able to produce and sell and the decisions of buyers about whether they wish or are able to continue consuming or holding or using the goods and services for sale.

The concept of competition supposes freedom in the market and freedom to enter or leave the market. Unless this freedom exists both in law and in practice, the social mechanism of the determination of prices is impaired or ceases to exist. The producers of a commodity can only discover how much to produce and what to produce if they are able to ascertain what consumers will pay them, and equally consumers can only discover what proportion of their assets they can use for buying a particular commodity or service. Furthermore, the market is a better means of achieving a match between production and consumption than any yet evolved.

All this seems obvious to anyone who has engaged in productive activity. Unfortunately what is obvious is not widely known or understood by the large number of people in our society who are not engaged in the production of goods and services whose prices are determined by market forces. In all societies an increasing proportion of people have incomes which are not determined either directly or indirectly in the market sector. Their incomes are derived from state revenues, and these revenues are obtained in three ways: by taxation which is the transfer of assets to the government from the owners by the use of power; by borrowing in the capital market, and by printing money or surrogates for money, which is a form of fraud inasmuch as it involves paying with counters which represent neither goods nor services. Only in the case of borrowing does the state make the owner of assets an offer which he or she *can* refuse. Taxes are paid because governments have the power (i.e. the force) to collect them; and inflation is a fraud endured because there is no law to prevent it and no agency to enforce such a law.

Incomes derived from state revenues, like subsidies from the same source, do not arise from bargains or exchanges of goods and services for goods and services. When very large numbers of people in a society rely in this way for their sustenance, even when they work at some administrative task or engage in planning or teaching, there exists in society a significantly large interest group whose members do not and cannot naturally have any knowledge of economic reality. Their self-interest expresses itself only as claims for more pay, better conditions, larger allowances and so on. The British economists Robert Bacon and Walter Eltis have revealed the shift from the productive market sector to non-productive employment in Britain over the past fifteen years. In 1975 the producers of goods and services in the market sector numbered 19,698,000 and they supported 5,270,000 people in non-productive employments plus 929,000 unemployed. Given present trends and assuming that the employment of people in the public service can be held at present levels, Bacon and Eltis predict that by 1982 18,700,000 will be supporting 5,270,000 in the non-market sector and 2,850,000 unemployed. (Robert Bacon and Walter Eltis, *Britain's Economic Problem: Too Few Producers*, Macmillan, London, 1978).

This being so, it is not difficult to see why there has been a serious diminution in understanding the economic realities of production and consumption and why knowledge of the rational allocation of resources and labour necessary in any effective economic system is breaking down.

Bacon and Eltis, like most economists, believe that the problems of the British economy can be put right by giving the government better advice based on better facts and better analysis. They do not see or understand the political problems involved. Governments do not take advice because it is good or scientific or true. Politicians are always obliged to do what their supporters demand: either to get into power or to stay there. When so many supporters of governments are dependent upon government for their incomes or for subsidies and when the productive sector is divided artificially by socialist and communist propaganda into antagonistic groups, it is little wonder that any British government, Conservative, Labour or Liberal, cannot find a sufficiently broad base of support to restore a market economy so that it can work effectively and freely.

The tax revolt in the United States is the most hopeful sign yet that free societies based on the principles of the market economy can check and reverse the trend towards collectivism. The tax revolt will lead to the re-establishment of limited government, i.e. government which makes rules and enforces them, but does not attempt to do what governments demonstrably cannot do efficiently or democratically, i.e. allocate labour and resources and determine the objectives of economic activity. If the power of governments to tax, to borrow and to manipulate the currency is curbed and constitutionally well defined, free enterprise, market economies will revive with all the benefits to mankind which experience has demonstrated this form of social organisation is capable of providing.

J. A. Kornberg was born in London on 16th August 1928. At the beginning of the war he was evacuated to Canada and the United States. While in the U.S.A. he was educated at the Bronx High School of Science, returning to the United Kingdom in 1943 he continued studies at Clifton College Bristol and Bude and Trinity College Cambridge where he graduated in 1950. Subsequently, he attended Bradford Technical College travelling extensively during this period in the U.S.A. and South America. In 1957 he obtained a Diploma in Business Management at L.S.E.

Mr. Kornberg entered the family business which eventually was absorbed by Lister & Company Limited Bradford of which he is now Joint Managing Director.

3

WHEN I WIN THE POOLS, I'LL...
by J. A. Kornberg

Today, we hear this expression everywhere: It is the archetypal cri-de coeur. Everybody wants things they can't afford and tragically, unless things change, they will never be able to afford, unless by coincidence, they win the pools, or get lucky on the horses, or at bingo or at the plethora of "Roman Holidays" that are provided to prevent the people "murmuring".

There was a time when people wanting things could see a possibility that through effort, ambition, drive, creativity they could acquire the things they wanted without waiting for their "number to come up".

However, with the society we have created these possibilities become less accessible momentarily. Why should this be so?

Every nation has its national "hang up" — the Germans understandingly, have an overwhelming fear of inflation. The U.S. of another "Great Crash", the Russians no doubt, have a fear of a return to serfdom — and we have a terror of massive unemployment.

It is said, "a scalded cat is frightened of cold water" and if we examine this old saw, we are saying that if something looks the same it *is* the same, so we react accordingly, although all the circumstances may be different. Therefore, we are attempting to use Keynes, who may or may not have drawn us up out of deep depression, as the prophet of our age, under the guise of Neo-Keynesism.

41

However, there was no OPEC in 1929.

Until approximately 200 years ago, the only source of "harnessable" energy was a horse. A man who owned a horse was automatically in a better class — i.e. cavalier or ritter. All this was changed by the release of hydro-carbon energy, first coal and then oil, and a greater egalitarianism emerged, which enabled far more people, in fact all people to partake of and use the products of "cheap" energy. The Western Industrial Societies and Japan adapted themselves and seized on cheap energy, and consequently although the West and Japan were the chief beneficiaries, the world enjoyed an era of unequalled prosperity. However, times have changed and those who have not been brought up on the philosophy either of Adam Smith or of Karl Marx are in control of the highest proportion of the world's resources of hydro-carbon energy, i.e. they are the new cavaliers or ritters, and they have no concept of "units of good" or egalitarianism, anti-trust, or even the distribution of wealth. Their only economic concept is of the concentration of wealth and its use to promote and dominate a world in their image. Since 1973, we have seen our world, the world we have known, slowly being suppressed by its hunger for cheap energy and the rising of the concept of expensive energy, not that energy sources are in any way diminishing — it still costs only a few cents to produce a barrel of oil which sells for about $11.

A dismantling of the OPEC cartel could make cheap energy available for the foreseeable future. Almost all the confrontations in the world today are due to the increase in the cost of energy, ranging from the Cod War to South American confrontations, and the disturbances in the Middle East and those to come.

When an established order is challenged, whether socially or economically, it is like a stone that is loosened and reveals the horrible things not previously allowed to see the light of day.

Up to now all efforts which have been made, whether determined or half-hearted, to re-establish balance, either in the form of EMS, conservation policies, over hasty development of alternative and expensive energy resources, appeasement of the new rich, charitable donations to the new poor, suppression of free enterprise, have been as has been said like — "rearranging the deck chairs on the Titanic".

Karl Marx envisioned the "fading away of the state". I don't think any of the bureaucrats ruling the so-called people's democracies would today care to be reminded of that phrase. Likewise Adam Smith's "Laissez Faire" hardly applies in an interventionist Western Democracy. And we know that the "Four Freedoms" are having a struggle to maintain themselves despite the timely presentation of President Carter's Human Rights Policy.

Therefore what we are seeing develop is Adam Smith's and Karl Marx's alternative philosophies of Capital coming under pressure from a Neo-Feudalism, emanating out of the Persian Gulf, which could well totally distort the shape of the Capitalist and Communist Worlds which continue to think everything will go on as before.

These new circumstances require totally new policies, if we are not to be cast back into a "Dark Age" even if it is "Electronic" to begin with.

Institutions that were founded and coped with past conditions will have to be revamped so much that they would not be recognisable to their founders. The bureaucratic Byzantine and Sassanid Empires fell in a few years to the Bedouin Arabs with their promise of little or no taxation and this eventually led to the first Dark Ages. Byzantine Rome was unable to afford to raise Citizen Armies, for all its wealth was squandered on an immoveable secular and religious bureaucracy.

Where does Free Enterprise come into all this?

Free Enterprise is the fundamental antagonist of bureaucracy. If bureaucracy with its fearful cost is going in the direction of destroying the world as we know it, so free enterprise with its productivity and flexibility will serve to save it and improve it. In this country there are some 700,000 free enterprises — if they alone could take on two extra workers we would have no unemployment.

Free Enterprises could then proliferate for there would be instead a demand for labour.

This is for openers!

Even Lenin turned to the NEP (New Economic Policy) before he died and if it had been allowed to grow, who knows what benefits Russia could have brought to the world. In the one democratic election held in Russia, the Liberals polled over 60% of the vote. The Communists less than 20%. Then there was the October Revolution. Nevertheless, the result of that one election shows that the craving for Freedom lies deep within the Russian Soul as indeed it does in all humanity.

An essential requirement for the New Free Society is the need to co-operate within a competitive system as opposed to the state of affairs today, where confrontation, working to rule, etc are the order of the day. It is essential to this Society that choice and incentive must be the key, not raffle tickets in lotteries. For it is important to give individuals the opportunity to retain more of that which has been earned instead of the earner giving it to others to spend or squander as they see fit.

A couple of years ago, an amusing little incident occurred which I think illustrates the muddle headedness of our present economic state. An employer, in South London discovered that a gold sovereign was legal tender for a £1 — although its market value then was £35.00. He paid his employees in gold sovereigns, thus a man earning £70.00 per week was paid two gold sovereign etc. As the legal value was £2.00 the employee had no tax to pay. Needless to say, the authorities were up in arms and the practice was discontinued. I recall being told that before the first world war, a working man was paid a gold sovereign a week with which to maintain his family. The employees mentioned above were paid two gold sovereigns with which to maintain their families. Therefore, it is arguable that the true inflation rate since the first war in gold, is only twice, whilst in paper money, we are all aware of what has happened.

Has all the economic unrest we have endured been to the benefit of *anyone*, other than those who have distorted the value of currency out of all proportion to its true worth? Except, of course, Government Printers and Paper Makers, and negotiators on both sides of industry.

I am not arguing for a return to the gold standard with all its deflationary and socially disturbing overtones, contrarily, I am saying that we have all been misled into believing that wages and conditions of employment have improved more in fact than they have improved. Gresham's Law — "bad money drives out good" — was if anything understated and did not take the issue far enough, for in the end bad local money will be replaced by good foreign money, provided by either civil or military despoilers.

Unfortunately we are becoming a nation of shabby bureaucrats with a constantly falling standard of living and as our cheap quality imports increase, our productivity deteriorates and our competitiveness in the world diminishes.

The Caste System in India largely developed, I believe, not from military conquest, but from economic causes, i.e. a demand for job security and job reservation, resulting in India becoming the ultimate crystallised society each man being "happy" with his lot however squalid. A lack of divine discontent other than dreams and spiritual longing, perpetuates a poverty that all the efforts of the modern world have hardly dented.

It could happen here, if the insistence on continued maintenance of outmoded crafts and skills is allowed to go unchallenged or with penalising new skills. It has been

45

said, that in Alexandria in the 1st Century AD, the concept of a steam powered turbine was mooted but eventually discarded for fear of social disturbance.

However, all is not lost. For all diseases there should be a diagnosis, prognosis and a cure. "Inflation is an infection of the economic system running out of control, it is necessary to find a cure, if we are ever to end it". Inflation, as we all know, is caused by too much money chasing too few goods. The cure must be in less money and more goods, i.e. healthy economic growth to reduce inflation provided there is not an excessive money supply.

How can this be achieved? I contend it is possible by first removing the constraints on trade within the country, then within the EEC and internationally. Initially, of course, there are monopolies (largely nationalised) oligopolies, (private) restrictive practices within industry and unions and of course bureaucratic interference, however well meant, in theory and intent.

In practice they distort economic activity i.e. the Employment Protection Act, which is known in industry as the Unemployment Protection Act, its provisions going so far as to inhibit the employment of labour, certainly by smaller companies, paradoxically those most ready to take on new labour.

Taxes should be reduced, "very high taxes reduce the revenue from taxation" (Professor Laffer — USC). Reduction of high tax rates could, after a period, increase revenue through increased effort and investment. Through our taxation system work has been penalised and leisure in all forms subsidised. Again according to Professor Laffer — "In a world of 100% taxation, no one would work, and in a world of no taxation, there would be no Government, only anarchy."

There should be huge cuts in P.S.B.R. (public sector borrowing requirement), and more public spending and investment should be transferred to the private sector where it would be handled with more efficiency, and greater profits would result in higher productivity and economic growth. Profits may, to the unaware, appear unattractive particularly in someone else's pocket, but in the meantime, more money is being extracted out of each person's pocket by the Taxation System, which must by its very nature be in perpetual deficit. Germany and Japan both cut their tax rates after the war in successive years heralding their economic miracles.

Politicians perpetually in fear of a fall in revenue increase taxes instead of reducing them, leading citizens to attempt to escape these higher taxes through "cash" economy in the "working" community and elaborate and expensive tax avoidance schemes in the business community, all of which continues the drain on the already unhealthy economy. Hence gambling is encouraged as a source of taxable income.

It is said that Faraday once demonstrated electricity to Disraeli, and after the demonstration Disraeli asked "What will be the use of this electricity?" to which Faraday replied — "For one thing sir, it will be very easy to tax". It is individuals who create wealth — and not Government! 14% of the U.S.S.R. is involved in agriculture — just about satisfying its requirements in food, as opposed to a mere 2% of the U.S. population, *a net exporter of food.*

We hear continual talk of better use of more leisure and less hours of work. Yet according to Robert Macnamara, the President of the World Bank, there are one thousand million people who do not have access to clean water. Is there not enough challenge in that appalling statistic to stimulate the creative impulse of Humanity? If these impulses can be released in a self disciplined manner, together with being mindful of the Biblical exhortation "The Earth is the Lord's and the fullness thereof" then there is the possibility that we may yet all win the Pools. God's plan for creation may be at the beginning.

Lord De L'Isle qualified as a Chartered Accountant in 1934, joined the staff of Barclays Bank in 1936 and stayed there till the outbreak of war. In 1939/40 he was in France and Belgium in the British Expeditionary Force and in 1943/44 he served in North Africa and Italy, and was awarded the V.C. after the Anzio landing in 1944.

He was elected to the House of Commons later that same year and in 1945 succeeded to his father's Peerage. Winston Churchill made him Secretary of State for Air in 1951. Five years later he re-entered business, becoming a managing director of Schweppes Ltd.

In 1961 he was appointed Governor-General of Australia and nearly four years later returned to Britain where he became Chairman of the Phoenix Assurance Company, relinquishing this post in 1978 on his 69th birthday. He was one of the founders of the National Association for Freedom, now The Freedom Association, of which he is Chairman.

4

FREE ENTERPRISE AND THE POLITICS OF POWER
by Lord De L'Isle

When in December 1941 the Japanese sank the American Pacific fleet in Pearl Harbour, we stood aghast. Only the very percipient were able to descry through the gloom the road to ultimate victory over the Axis powers.

As I write, it is now our turn. Britain is the target of a vicious attack, not by an external enemy, but by a small but militant section of our own people who are attempting to hold the whole community under threat in order to gain their ends while, in the process, they deliberately set constitutional government at nought.

As with the Japanese, so with the larger unions, the menace could have been foreseen and the defences alerted. But political leaders, especially when facing the prospect of an election, rarely take the risk of forcing public opinion to face the ugly facts of life.

Indeed, before Pearl Harbour President Roosevelt had repeatedly assured his nation that he would never lead it into war. Fortunately for the world, even before the blow was struck, he had the good sense to realise that his country would be unable to avoid war, and so had begun his preparations to fight it. Although unrealised at the time, he had already begun to bend his bow when the war started.

However, despite the President's sense of anticipation, the Allied victory over the Axis powers would not have been gained had not the will to achieve it been hardened by the shock of defeat and disaster.

Now in our moment of crisis, our national stiuation must be clearly and realistically analysed. First we must take a hard and dispassionate look at the processes which have brought our country to the brink of disaster.

The first essential for enlightenment on the road back to freedom is that in a ruthless age men and women will go to all lengths to gain their ends and will utterly disregard the rules, conventions and values which once set bounds to the field of civilised political controversy. Once we have grasped this reality we can comprehend how it has come about that the very government which conceded to the Trade Unions the right legally to assail the fabric of our economy, and to disrupt our ordered life with impunity, should find itself begging those same Unions not to use against itself weapons which it had put into their hands.

With a new understanding of power we can see that the long term aim of the Trade Union Movement has been not merely to subdue the opposition, if and when in office, but to undermine all constituted authority in Britain. Why hesitate when the omens are so good.

The second essential for an understanding of the discontents which now afflict us is the comprehension that for more than a generation the political establishment of this country has, with important exceptions, succeeded in bringing about a continuous extension of the areas in which government operates. The public professions of individual members of that establishment vary according to the particular colour in the political spectrum which they wear on their coats. Their actions, however, when in positions of power or influence, are based on a shared conviction that public men and politicians do really have the prescience and the expertise to enable them to plan and control the national economy over a very wide field and in great detail. All such people are united in hating and mistrusting the market economy. This has been very serviceable to the Left.

The third essential is to acknowledge that when power to act has been regained, to be effective this must be based on an intelligible political theory, capable of being developed in popular terms. For without a theme song of its own, a party must inevitably be compelled to sing to a tune of its own opponents. This has been the case here since World War II, and even before.

Basic assumptions must be changed or the deprivations and humiliations being suffered by our people will not in themselves be sufficient to alter fixed habits of mind. The unpopularity of a particular government may not alone effect a revulsion from the policies which have so obviously failed.

In the foregoing paragraphs I have attempted to outline he principal factors which have to be reckoned with in our struggle to re-establish freedom. It is only by an understanding of the forces which are ranged against us that we can hope to achieve success in our efforts. Our opponents, too, have their difficulties in the resentments which the exercise of excessive power arouses.

But we cannot rely, as I have tried to point out, solely on the forces of reaction. The other side are just as much aware of this as we are, but they are confident that with the levers of power firmly in their hands they can afford to disregard any manifestations of popular disapproval.

I do not propose in this article to discuss the general philosophy of freedom or to sketch even in outline a plan of campaign whereby we may restore and enlarge it. In a book on Private Enterprise it is sufficient to point out that private enterprise operating within a market economy is one of the principal supports of a free society. It should be plain that our discomforts, shared by almost all, should be used insistently to illustrate the superiority of the market economy.

We should point, as well, to the sound morality of a system of personal responsibility and of individual choice which a free market promotes, and we must underpin the framework of freedom by reference to an articulate theory.

In the past, advocates of a free market have had to contend with a formidable flood of criticism founded largely upon the supposed higher moral tone of a planned society. Today the boot is on the other foot. It is the planners and collectivists who are on the defensive because they have claimed so much and have performed so ill, not only in Britain but wherever collectivism has gained the ascendancy. The idols have fallen, but nevertheless the idolaters are still fervently practising their rites within the citadels of power.

So we must, with even greater fervour, spread afresh the good news that we are not doomed for ever to be part of a command society, and that private enterprise operating under competition is an essential pre-condition of the system of freedom. With such perceptions firmly based on evidence which is now incontrovertible, we can look our enemies boldly in the face and do battle with them from positions of advantage.

We have the shield of truth and the sword of conviction for the encouragement of our own forces, which it must be remembered comprise not only the militant but the hesitant.

We must speak with assurance, for we know that "if the trumpet give an uncertain sound, who shall prepare himself to the battle?"

Some comments on Power
from *Bachman's Book of Freedom Quotations*

LORD ACTON
Power tends to corrupt and absolute power corrupts absolutely.
(*Historical Essays and Studies*)

ARMEN A. ALCHIAN
The man who enters political life to restrain the growth of public ownership, publicly-operated agencies and services, will find that he must dismantle his major sources of power and wealth once he is in office. His survival chances in political office will diminish compared to those of another man taking the opposite position.
(*Pricing and Society*)

ANON
There are two pursuits, love and power, but no man can have both.
(*Inscription by Roman centurion found in Libyan desert*)

CHARLES d'AVENANT
Custom, that unwritten law,
By which the people keep even kings in awe.
(*Circe*)

FRANCIS BACON
It is a strange desire to seek power and to lose liberty.
(*Of Great Place*)

WALTER BAGEHOT
The best reason why Monarchy is a strong government is, that it is an intelligible government. The mass of mankind understand it, and they hardly anywhere in the world understand any other.
(*The English Constitution: The Monarchy*)

EDVARD BENES
The philosophy of power is barbaric, inhuman and absurd philosophy.

Michael Ivens has been Director of Aims, the free enterprise organisation, since January 1971

Director of the Foundation for Business Responsibilities (formerly Industrial Educational and Research Foundation) since 1966.

Joint founder and member of Management Committee, The Freedom Association.

A founder of the Working Together Campaign; Director for the first year.

Joint Editor of *Twentieth Century* (1966-1973).

Books written or edited:

Practice of Industrial Communication
Which Way? — Thirteen Choices Facing Britain
The Case for Capitalism
Case Studies in Management
Case Studies in Human Relations, Productivity and Organisation
Case Studies in Marketing, Finance and Control
Industry and Values
Prophets of Freedom and Enterprise
Bachman's Book of Freedom Quotations

Lectures and Broadcasting:

Lecture tour of Latin America under the auspices of the British Council and the South American Association for Scientific Management. Also lectured in United States and Europe. Frequent broadcaster.

5

FREEDOM NEEDS FREE ENTERPRISE
by Michael Ivens

More and more this question is being asked in Britain these days: what are the conditions suitable for freedom in a modern industrial State?

We like to hold this country up as a model of freedom for the rest of the world. This concept of ourselves is still broadly valid. Nevertheless, we are now one of the most highly State-owned countries outside the Communist bloc, and the process is accelerating. It needs only simple arithmetic to show that the trend in our political system for Labour Governments to move five steps towards total nationalisation, while succeeding Conservative administrations take only a faltering half-step backwards, must lead to a State society by the end of the century.

There is a direct relationship between freedom of enterprise and the broader freedoms. True freedom can only exist if there is a market economy. Free enterprise, in turn, can only function efficiently in a climate of freedom. That is why we have cause to be alarmed at the way free enterprise has been gradually squeezed out by a combination of fiscal policies and the expansion of State ownership. Alongside of this is the phenomenal outpouring of legislation which, however well-intentioned, must inevitably build up to a point where it restricts individual as well as corporate freedom.

Before I consider some of the requisites for safeguarding freedom, let us look at causes of the present anxieties.

First, the inflation of the last few years has produced a great deal of insecurity. That is not surprising. It is a general accompaniment of inflation. The insecurity is real, and when the inflation is accompanied by high and selective taxes, people feel that their feet are slipping down the social slopes.

Then we have the avalanche of legislation in the last few years. Both the major parties have made their contribution to this. Members of Parliament are fond of mentioning the relatively few shelves that hold our collection of laws up to 1900, and the vast collection of documents since which dwarfs the efforts of the earlier centuries.

Parliament can quite easily put aside laws and practices that we value, and unwilling Members of Parliament can be driven into doing so by the rules of interparty warfare.

Sydney Webb once said that our trade unions had a legal status whose privilege could only be equalled by those of the monasteries in the Middle Ages. They are now adding to this the force and power of the barons, and it is their influence on government that is worrying the man and woman in the street.

We look to the government for protection against the strong. In the 19th century the Conservative Party recognised that it should not be the party of business, and this was essential to provide a counterweight to the growing power of the capitalists. But now that Labour Governments seem to be married to the trade unions, the citizen looks elsewhere for his protection. If he cannot turn to the politician, then he looks to the law.

The fact that government has seemed to give priority to the claims of one vested interest in society has warmed up the debate on whether Britain needs a Bill of Rights, and who should see that it is implemented. We cannot afford any longer to be complacent — still less proud — about not having a written constitution. The consequence of not having one is that Parliament can make up the constitution and interpret constitutional rights as it goes along, to suit itself. If we ever overcame the hurdles that many elements in Parliament would put up against a Bill of Rights providing many of the safeguards one looks for in a written constitution, we would have to be careful that Parliament could not lightly meddle with it. This, given the mood of Parliament which Lord Hailsham has described with some justification as an elective dictatorship, would be hard to achieve.

It would not be easy to get agreement on the contents of a Bill of Rights. It would be better if it could be produced by agreement between the main parties, though in practice it may have to be introduced by one.

Certainly it should be preceded by a referendum. And it is not going to be much use by itself unless we have something like a supreme court to see that it is implemented. The Soviet constitution is full of glowing words, but it doesn't help the dissenters. In the long run, of course, Parliament can always have the judges marched off to prison — but then the democratic game is over anyhow.

Although I am for a Bill of Rights, it does seem to me to be very dangerous indeed to see the conditions for freedom as being resolved by its introduction. The conditions are much wider and deeper. Here is it necessary for me to state my political philosophy (too many statements are put forward from a concealed position). It is that of an Inverted Marxist.

Marx seems to me to have the great merit of having brought home the relationship between the form of the economy, the methods of production, distribution and exchange, and the cultural values of the society. He grasped, for example, that capitalism was making culture and communication international rather than provincial. He was not, of course, the first. Many centuries before, the great Arabic historian Ibn Khaldun produced a map of accompanying human changes of an economy.

But Marx got it wrong. I am sure that in an industrial society it is necessary to have diffused power and ownership in order to have the freedoms we value. In other words, just as Marx stood Hegel on his head, so it is necessary to stand Marx on his, and recognise that free enterprise and individual ownership are necessary to freedom. And, contrariwise, that a State society is an unfree one.

We do, of course, talk a lot about diffusing, delegating and decentralising power. But "property" is a repressed word in the debate. Yet — let us take some examples.

We talk of an Englishman's home being his castle. The freedom is, of course, relative. Bulldozers, government orders and acts of God can demolish the largest pile. But his property rights do act as a bulwark — even his renting rights. It is hard to have the same feeling about a council flat. Here his right to keep pets or grandmothers, or paint his outer walls eccentrically, or to introduce a sauna bath, are by no means assured. The sense of freedom is different. It is all too true that where everybody owns everything, nobody owns anything.

Property — the right of individual ownership — is essential in the case of newspapers. The dangers of their being owned and capitalised by the State are too obvious, and most people would reject the idea that they should be. Individual ownership is necessary for newspapers to be able to produce their own independent policies and comment. But there are threats to the traditional independence of our newspapers. Ferocious over-manning and resistance to technological progress bring the threat of closures, and the possibility of the State injecting money and shareholders.

If market forces drive a newspaper out, that is a different matter. It can be assumed that it is no longer filling a need, and there is always the possibility that someone will come along with a new and different newspaper to try and capture the dead paper's readership. But we have seen an example in The Times of a newspaper which had its niche and was beginning to pay its way being forced to the wall by the inflexible approach to production needs — we will put it in no more sinister terms than that — of some of its unions. In an era when government is so anxious to please the unions, the danger immediately arose of the Government stepping in "to save jobs", perhaps by the National Enterprise Board putting in money to establish the foundations of a press empire. The taxpayer's money had already been used in an attempt to bolster up the Scottish Daily News — an object lesson, if ever there was one, that jobs in the long run depend on satisfying the customer, that even State money cannot make a moribund enterprise viable if it has lost its market.

Union power in the press has introduced a rash of censorship, most of it unobserved by — or concealed from — the public. Even an issue of Hansard reporting a House of Lords debate on press freedom was censored for nine days with the excuse that it was because of an "industrial dispute". A glance at the Communist Party's 1977 *The British Road for Socialism* throws up another threat — the call for the nationalisation of newsprint and printing ink.

If the State — and the unions — got control of these two industries, it would be very simple for them to "black" newspapers they disapproved of. The drive to introduce a closed shop into newspapers, with a possible ban on freelances, or on freelances without union tickets, sometimes backed up by left-controlled public authorities banning information to people without union cards, or to newspapers which are the target of "industrial action", is another threat. One reason why so much of the censorship and harmful practices imposed on newspapers by union pressures are unknown to the public is that they have gone largely unreported in the press. And thereby management, by playing it safe and acquiescing in concealing what goes on, has provided an illustration of how freedom can be eroded by a combination of corporatism and weakness.

Television and radio are, so far, less under attack, though the Trotskyists are looking eagerly at the staff of commercial radio stations. The BBC is, of course, an historically outstanding example of a semi-government corporation achieving splendid standards of balance and lack of political bias — though it should not be forgotten how the advent of independent television forced on the BBC the disciplines of a competitive commercial market which it had to accept if it wanted to keep its viewers. People tend to forget nowadays the era when the BBC insisted on giving listeners what it thought they ought to get, rather than what they may have preferred. No doubt Governments will fight to prevent commercial television or radio stations having independent political views — but the American experience of diffused ownership and independence is safer.

One should not just single out television and radio for anxiety. The same situation applies to our State education and the National Health Service. Both have had successes, and education, in particular, has reflected the splendid standards of non-partisanship in a State enterprise, which is the legacy of the Victorians. Here again tax policies have made it more difficult for independent and religious schools to survive. The idea of teaching as a political act — though fortunately not applying to most teachers — has nevertheless crept in.

In the National Health Service we have seen private wards closed, not because of Government decision, but because of pressure through strikes by cleaners, cooks and porters. We have also had the case of the psychiatrist who alleged that nurses had beaten up patients. The result was that the local health authority suspended the psychiatrist from duty! This ironic story would have caused a public outcry a few years ago. It has inspired very little interest or indignation.

In order to have checks and safeguards, it is essential in a democracy to be able to choose services other than those provided by the State. Too often the fundamental argument for this is seen, even by its supporters, as being in terms of social advantage or conspicuous consumption. But the existence of private services — whether in schools or medicine or health (or building, for that matter) — is an insurance that the State or trade unions may not alone decide what is education, or what are desirable health services, or whether one is a fit person to have a home.

One argument for independent schools can be seen when you consider the total impossibility of their existing in countries like the Soviet Union and China. They would be an affront to the State concept of culture and the individual.

One of William James' most moving essays was on *A Certain Blindness in Human Beings*. We often fail to sympathise imaginatively with the needs of others. I reflect on James' essay when I consider the mutual misunderstandings of businessmen and intellectuals. Here there is considerable "blindness".

Intellectuals can see quite easily the need for property-freedoms applying to the production of books, newspapers, films and works of art. They realise that individual innovation, creation and ownership are essential. They do not see the imaginative needs of the businessmen, and especially of the first-generation entrepreneur, who in many ways has a kinship to the artist. The entrepreneur is totally absorbed in the creation of a product or service. He puts his *self* into it. He may not have the tidiness of the professional manager; he may sometimes have the irritating egoism which is not unknown in the artist. Intellectuals and those who see their lives in terms of words and comment rather than actions find it difficult to imagine that the entrepreneur's satisfaction may be considerable in the task of creating goods and services, in moving them around the world, in devising new things and methods.

It is this lack of imaginative sympathy that makes for the creation of policies of nationalisation, State control and bureaucracy which frustrate the entrepreneur in a larger way of business as well as the small and independent businessman.

Of course the businessman is not always a paragon of imaginative sympathy. He may be strong on freedom for activity; he may, in contrast, be illiberal on social and sexual innovations, on dress, on new political views. Very often he can be a notable example of Eysenck's conservative hard-headedness.

The State as the banker, moneylender and executioner combined has had a ferocious effect on industry. The history since the war of alternating threats and pats had the same effect as those experiments on wretched mice which have sometimes been allowed to eat the cheese and sometimes given shocks when they touch it; like the mice, the businessmen lie down and refuse to budge. Moreover they are often unwilling to argue publicly about Government policies, or to criticise them, for fear of retaliation in monetary kind.

There also comes a time when a threatened industry lies low. They are aware that some steel directors who fought too hard and long against steel nationalisation had short shrift when the industry was taken over.

A disturbing product of the overkill of legislation we have had is the proliferation of quangos — quasi-autonomous national government organisations — with the immense power of patronage they represent for Ministers to reward people who support them or do not speak out of turn. Appointment to quangos, of course, also confers considerable power and privilege on appointees, and some trade union leaders — as sometimes do their wives and relatives — enjoy high incomes and many useful perks in the way of tax-free expenses from multiple mem-

bership of boards, tribunals, commissions and commit-
tees. The existence of these bodies obviously represents
such wide-ranging scope for patronage as to pose a potential threat to readiness to show free and democratic disagreement on principles with the people who have the
power to exercise it.

As national and local government control and ownership expands, individual freedom must inevitably diminish. In fact Marx himself well understood this, and
associated the opposite — the progress of capitalism —
with increasing democracy. He saw that a condition of
the development of democracy was freedom for the capitalist. There is nothing illogical about this. The early capitalists had to free themselves from restrictions which
were the antithesis of a libertarian and democratic
society — absolute monarchy and its rigidly-organised
structure of bureaucrats, monopolies reserved for the
ruler or his favourites, and orders of precedence; landed
interests, and even the Church.

The greatest drive for liberty, and the greatest achieve-
ments in that drive, in our history have coincided with
the development of capitalism. The Reform Bills which
extended the franchise to all adults were pushed through
in the last century at a time when capitalists were taking
over political, as well as economic, power, from the old
landed gentry. What an irony it is that universal suffrage
has been used to give power to ideologies which are
opposed to capitalism and inclined to authoritarianism.

But it is a characteristic of succeeding generations not
to appreciate the worth of what their elders handed on to
them. In the case of those who developed capitalism, that
worth is beyond price. The ordinary citizen of a western
country — even those classified as "poor" — has a standard of living that would have been beyond the wildest
imagining of his ancestors. That it is also far in advance
of the standard in countries where capitalism has been
ejected is not without significance, either.

Among the many freedoms capitalism has brought, not least are freedom of choice and freedom to move. There is a vast variety of goods in the shops, and services which add to the quality of life, to choose from. The potential range of trades, and jobs within those trades, for people to work in, would have been inconceivable in the rigid societies of the past where each had his allotted occupation. Not only in the past, but in some Marxist societies today.

Under capitalism — unlike Marxism — people are free to choose whether to gain their living by working for somebody else, or by going into business on their own account. Because so many people have been free to back their own faith in the service they could offer, or an idea, or something they could make, we have the variety and abundance of choices we enjoy.

A by-product of this freedom is a mobility in society unlike anything in the past (although Britain has been a relatively mobile society since the early middle ages. Class-consciousness and class mobility go together). This is true not only in the social sense — where freedom to move from one layer to another has given us members of the "upper classes" whose very recent roots were in Coronation Street rather than among privileged invitees at Coronations — but in industry and business. A man can still earn wealth and a seure station in life by his own ability. And Professor David Granick has shown in his studies "The Red Executive" and "The European Executive" that it is much easier to work one's way up to the top from the shopfloor in British industry than in France, Germany, the United States — or in the Soviet Union, where top management need both formal and political qualifications. In Britain only about half of top managers have formal qualifications, and a survey shows that one-fifth of all British directors left school at the age of 15. A high proportion, therefore, must have got where they were by their own merit and practical ability.

Capitalism is by no means flawless. No human creation is. It may carry with it inequalities; some people will make it, others will go down. But it has produced enough materially to provide subsistence, and better, even for those who do not make it. Non-capitalist societies may also make provision to prevent anyone starving, but they do it at such a cost in freedom and wellbeing for the greater number that only the deliberately blind could fail to note that the freedoms and quality of life enjoyed by the majority of us in the west are associated with a free enterprise, capitalist system.

Perhaps the greatest dangers to capitalism come from two quarters. One is from the people who practise free enterprise themselves — not because what they do and how they do it is in any way less than creditable, but because they do not stand up for the system. Many of them are not very good at putting forward the arguments in favour of free enterprise; some do not see that being too ready to accept government participation is the beginning of the end.

The other danger to free enterprise is that most people take it for granted. True, there are some for whom it is a cause, but generally speaking the idea of free enterprise doesn't fire the blood or inspire martyrs. Communism and socialism, on the other hand, have something of the character of substitute-religions. Their attraction to the young is that they offer a commitment, something to man the barricades over and to make sacrifices for. Free enterprise can never be a substitute-religion; it doesn't aspire to take over the whole of a person's life. Yet it is part of a way of life, and it is one of the keys to a good life.

People who practise free enterprise must become better at saying why it is the best. Like those who oppose it, they must use every opportunity to expound what they believe in. The essential message is that freedom needs free enterprise.

Harry Welton in his previous role of Director of Information and Research was responsible for all the publications circulated by the Economic League. His other activities included the briefing of industrialists, trade unionists, MPs and the Press on the aims and methods of subversive groups operating in industry. Since relinquishing this post he has been retained by the League in a consultative capacity.

Mr. Welton, who is well known here and abroad as a lecturer on the problems of industry, is the author of three books:

"The Third World War" (trade and industry — the new battle-ground);
"The Trade Unions, the Employers and the State"
"The Unnecessary Conflict".

He has also written several booklets including "The Agitators" (a standard booklet which has been issued in revised form on three occasions).

He has appeared on BBC television programmes including "Panorama" and "Man Alive" and, because of his knowledge of the subversive organisations, he has also been interviewed on TV on several occasions when the activities of these organisations have been in the news.

His work in the field of industrial relations has taken him to such parts of the world as the United States, West Indies, East Africa, India, Pakistan and Western Europe.

6

WHY FREE ENTERPRISE
by Harry Welton

It is a sad commentary on modern political life when those of us who support free enterprise are more than ever conscious of the need to defend it against attacks that could be lethal.

Yet despite the left-wing claim that Britain needs more "socialism", the facts prove that this does not represent the opinion of workers in this country or for that matter in others where the right to choose still exists.

There is abundant evidence that the majority of Britons lack enthusiasm for any further extension of nationalisation and prefer the free enterprise method of running our industrial and commercial enterprises.

For example, a public survey carried out in 1976 covering workers in the mining, manufacturing and construction industries revealed that no less than 86 per cent of those interviewed considered it important for them to live in a free enterprise society.

Consider too the reactions of the main unions organising bank workers to the proposal that major sectors of their industry be taken over by the state. They demonstrated in the most forthright manner that they wanted none of it.

Of particular interest was the attitude of the National Union of Bank Employees. When examining the nationalisation proposals, this union posed three down-to-earth questions.

(1) Would they benefit the bank employees?

(2) Would they benefit the industry and its customers?

(3) Would they benefit the economy as a whole?

The answers led, inevitably, to the conclusion that no evidence had been produced to justify nationalisation from any of these standpoints. Further, the NUBE General Secretary expressed the hope that other associations — political or otherwise — would adopt the same approach.

It is unfortunately a hope that has no chance of fulfilment as far as left-wingers in both the political and industrial sides of the Labour movement are concerned. Their dogmas are too deeply entrenched for any real change of heart. They will, if given the chance, establish a complete socialist state in Britain whether we want it or not.

By contrast support for free enterprise owes nothing to dogma. It is based upon a factual assessment of industrial and commercial progress in the democratic nations and comparison with conditions in "socialist" countries.

It is obvious that over the years millions of people have similarly assessed the situation with the same results. Throughout the ages, large numbers of men and women have been prepared to hitch their wagons to a star and seek a new life in some far off part of their own or some other country.

They were prepared to face fearsome dangers and suffer severe hardship. They travelled with more hope than certainty about the prospects at their chosen destinations.

Modern emigrants are far better informed. They know more about conditions in different parts of the world. They travel just as hopefully, but not as blindly, as the old pioneers.

Where do most of them choose to go? Almost invariably they opt for a democratic country where free enterprise still functions. They shun the so-called socialist countries where everything in sight has been nationalised. There are not, and never have been queues of people seeking admission into countries where Marxists rule.

As one prominent left-wing propagandist sadly admitted — free enterprise countries have to pass laws to stop too many people coming in, while "socialist" countries pass strict laws to stop their people getting out.

The facts speak for themselves — the highest standards of living combined with the greatest degree of individual liberty are found in countries where free enterprise is still allowed to function.

This is beyond contradiction. The links between prosperity and free enterprise are as clear now as they ever were. It is not the "socialist" countries behind which Britain now lags in the standard-of-living league table. Those who have left us behind — temporarily I hope — are nations in which free enterprise is encouraged by governments, the people, and, let it be noted, the trade unions too.

That life in Britain improved immeasurably under free enterprise is a fact that cannot sensibly be denied. If anyone who died early this century could see how most of us live today, after suffering such disasters as the two most destructive wars in history, a general strike and innumerable financial and economic crises, he would wonder what we were complaining about.

He would see that our standard of living has improved beyond the wildest dreams of his contemporaries and that, despite the difficult, potentially dangerous problems with which we are faced, Britain is one of the best countries in which to live and work.

He would see most of us using in our everyday lives goods and services which, a comparatively short time ago, were not available even to the richest of people. Certainly he would echo the words of the late Lord Feather — formerly chairman of the TUC — who described our standard of living as "little short of a miracle".

This did not happen by accident or good luck. Nor did so-called "socialist" solutions play any part. The driving force was free enterprise through which the initiative, enterprise, inventive genius and the energies of the British people were allowed to function with the minimum of intervention by the state.

It is this last vital point that socialist politicians cannot or will not grasp. For instance, when Mr. Callaghan stated quite correctly that in his lifetime the standard of living in this country had risen to a degree unknown when he was young, he attributed this to the operations of the Welfare State.

As another old socialist George Bernard Shaw once remarked in a different context "If you believe that you will believe anything". The Welfare State did not and could not bring this about. It is concerned with the redistribution, not the creation of wealth. It puts the emphasis on spending not earning.

Improved social services do not cause greater national affluence. They result from it. Adequate provision for the needy is not possible in a poverty-stricken country. If it was there would be no such thing as hunger or deprivation in any part of the world.

We have a Welfare State because free enterprise created the wealth that has enabled us to take care of those who, for one reason or another, cannot adequately fend for themselves. If we want still further to improve our social services — and most of us do — then more wealth will have to be created.

The truth needs to be shouted from the housetops that it is industry and commerce not politicians, that enable us to pay the country's bills, and therefore make possible the housing, health, education, welfare benefits and everything else that makes up our standard of living. Jonathan Swift, the author of "Gulliver's Travels", got it right when he said:

"Whoever could make two ears of corn or two blades of grass to grow upon a spot of ground where only one grew before would deserve better of mankind and do more essential service to his country than the whole race of politicians put together."

Britain would be a more prosperous country if this truth was understood and acted upon by all politicians. Their role should not be to poke sticks into the free enterprise clock so that they can complain about imperfect time-keeping, but to concentrate their efforts on creating conditions in which those engaged in industry and commerce can more efficiently do their job.

One can forgive early pioneers of nationalisation. They had little other than their hearts to guide them. But there is no excuse for present day "socialists" who ignore the lessons of history and will, if we let them, extend nationalisation to the point where all of us operate under state control.

Nationalisation has demonstrably failed to fulfil the promises of its advocates. It has not made goods and services more plentiful and cheaper. It has not resulted in better services to customers. It has not brought about improved industrial relations. It has not led to greater job security.

Further those who want the state to become the universal producer and provider should ponder one of the important lessons of history that any government powerful enough to do everything for us is also powerful enough to do anything it likes to us.

The economic answer to the question "Why free enterprise?" is quite simply that it has proved to be the best way so far devised of producing and selling goods and services in ever-increasing quantities and varieties.

It is the private enterprise sector of industry that produces nearly all the goods and services necessary to pay our way in the world and, by doing so, finances the importation of food, raw materials and other products essential to our standard of living. It is also the private enterprise sector that is compelled to work under constant attacks from those whose ambition is to destroy it and to turn Britain into a Marxist state. To paraphrase Jonathan Swift, they are doing their utmost to cause one ear of corn and one blade of grass to grow where two previously grew.

Here are two statements made by men of long experience in the trade union movements of their respective countries. First this is what the late Mr. Ray Gunter — speaking as Minister of Labour in a socialist government — said more than 10 years ago:

> "It is only the expansion of our industry that can in the end prevent even more unemployment. I do wish so many of our comrades would stop equating profits with incest or lechery.
> " If you have a profitable industry you have the means for further investment and further development and more jobs. If you have an unprofitable industry you do not expand and you do not get more jobs."

That made sense then and it still does.

More recently, in October 1978, Walter Sickert, a top union leader in West Germany, spelled out a message that everyone in Britain should note and act upon before it is too late.

Herr Sickert, who started his working life as an apprentice toolmaker and is now chairman of the German trade unions in Berlin, refuted any suggestion that the higher standards of living now obtaining in his country had anything to do with the superiority of the German worker. He is, he said, just as lazy or just as industrious as the British. What then is the secret? As Herr Sickert put it:

> "You have to realise that we have achieved our success by setting ourselves up as the strongest promoters of the free market capitalist system in which we work."

Herr Sickert also made the point that with Communism at their doorstep, German trade unionists are in a better position than ours to assess the consequences of a left-wing take over. He said:

> "We here in Berlin, particularly, can see what it means to slide to the left to collective socialism because if we are ever in doubt we can cross into East Berlin and see for ourselves the difference between their life and ours."

That sums it up. Be sure of this. If Britain is to resume its role in the world as a prosperous high wage economy we must rapidly become a high productivity economy. In a democratic society it is only free enterprise that can achieve this.

Sir Frank Taylor was born January 1905 in Hadfield, Derbyshire and left school at the age of thirteen, then attended night school, and in 1921 with a modest bank loan built two houses in Blackpool — intended for his family — which he was persuaded to sell at a profit.

In 1935 Taylor Woodrow Limited — established in 1930 — became a public company; the contracting and civil engineering aspects were developed and the Group began expanding both at home and overseas, first in North America, then Africa and then, in the early 'fifties, in the Middle East. Today, the group is still heavily committed in those areas.

In July 1973 Salford University conferred an Honorary D.Sc upon FT (as he is widely known) and the Chancellor at that time, HRH Prince Philip, Duke of Edinburgh, officiated. On January 1st 1974, the day that he formally relinquished the chairmanship of the Taylor Woodrow Group whilst retaining the managing directorship, FT became Sir Frank Taylor in the New Year Honours.

A passionate believer in free enterprise and the freedom, with responsibility, of the individual, Sir Frank takes every opportunity to air his views and this honest, forthright approach was recognised in 1976 when the National Association for Freedom nominated him as their 'Man of the Year.'

Lady Taylor began her career as a 16-year-old copy typist with Taylor Woodrow during the Second World War, worked her way through the ranks to become FT's secretary and today sits on the Group's parent board and on that of Taylor Woodrow Homes Limited. Although Sir Frank has announced his intention of relinquishing the Group managing directorship in June 1979 he will retain his seat on the board and become the Group's first president as well, of course, as its Founder.

7

THE THREAT OF NATIONALISATION
by Sir Frank Taylor

Judge J. P. Curran observed as long ago as 1790 "It is the common fate of the indolent to see their rights become a prey to the active. The condition upon which God hath given liberty to man is eternal vigilance, which condition if he break servitude is at once the consequence of his crime, and the punishment of his guilt."

That extremely sensible assessment of the price of freedom, made as it was nearly 200 years ago, is if anything even more valid today, but perhaps it is easier to absorb if we translate it into the modern idiom. The word "indolent" means "indisposed to activity" or, if you like, idle, but I do not think it is because people are idle that their basic freedoms have been, and continue to be, eroded. It is because they are usually so busy doing other things that they do not have time to safeguard their rights, or, even more often perhaps, because they don't fully recognise a threat to their rights until it is too late. They are, sadly, prepared to leave the fight to others, often with disastrous consequences.

How do you maintain constant vigilance? Well first of all you must find time to take an interest in current affairs, not entirely political, and commit to memory or better still, filing cabinet, items of news which disturb you. Simultaneously, sound out your friends and business acquaintances on their views and, if necessary, make joint representations on issues of concern. Above all, listen to the opposing view and analyse it so that you are in a position to destroy it when the time comes. That, incidentally, is how the construction and civil engineering industries drew their strength in the entirely honourable Campaign Against Building Industry Nationalisation (CABIN) but more on that topic later. And it was probably an absence of that communication and liaison which sealed the fate of those industries now owned by the State. An absence of what we, in Taylor Woodrow, call teamwork.

The forces acting against free enterprise and the freedom of the individual are formidable. If you turn the pages of almost any national newspaper on any given day you will find examples of serious threat to or erosion of these basic rights and I suppose the most frightening aspect is that these cunning, subversive elements who seek to destroy all that is worthy in civilised society and replace it with Communist totalitarianism are mobilised around the world, not just in Great Britain.

In Britain, there can be little doubt that the fundamental cause of our ever-declining economic status in recent years is due to one thing alone — industrial relations, or more correctly, lack of them — and this under a Socialist Government. Similarly, and it must be said, a marked decline in moral values can also be blamed firmly on Socialist dogma and trade union muscle. Who, for example, has lulled elements of the public into believing, without question, that the State should provide and that they should be cosseted from the cradle to the grave? Who has taught them that rigorous self-denial to find the money for the private education of one's children is a heinous crime? Who has introduced a state of affairs whereby a man or woman has every right to join a trade union but no right whatsoever to opt out of union membership without losing his or her job? And probably never getting another in that field?

But back to the economic problem. For the fourth successive year the Government imposed, in 1978, "pay guidelines". For the fourth time it told employers what maximum percentage increase they may pay to their workers in a 12-month period. What it didn't say was how, after four years in which earnings increases failed to come anywhere near increases in the cost of living index, they were supposed to persuade their workers to accept a five per cent increase. Neither has the Government ever attempted, or even offered to try, to force militant trade unions to keep their claims within the pay guidelines. If, however, the employer is forced to bow to union pressure and pay over the odds then the Government imposes sanctions against *him and not against the union concerned.*

How are these sanctions applied? Well in the case of a British company which operates overseas, bringing in much-needed foreign currency which assists the UK balance of payments, the Government will blithely withdraw any Export Credit Guarantees which that company may have. In consequence, and unless the company can find other suitable sureties, it loses contracts which might be worth millions of pounds. Similarly, of course, and without those valuable orders, the blacklisted company may find that it has to reduce its workforce or even close altogether, leading to further strife and misery.

In the case of an employer in the United Kingdom who breaches the pay guidelines — whether under union pressure or otherwise and it is rarely otherwise since most are realistic about the nation's economy — the Government could, for example, prevent that company from tendering for its own, or local authority contracts. Or it could prevent the employer from raising prices to finance wage increases which he had no option but to pay because of militant union pressure. Or it could, in the case of the Ford Motor Company, for example, which in the autumn of 1978 lost millions as a result of a prolonged dispute consider blacking Ford cars for Ministers, Under-

77

Secretaries and the host of Whitehall minions who ride around at public expense, and instruct local authorities not to buy Ford cars and commercial vehicles. In the event the Government's odious sanctions proposals against employers were thrown out by Parliament in December 1978. But doubt not that, given the chance, they would seek to reimpose such harmful measures.

There are, also, two other aspects of Government pay policy to which I must refer and these are areas where ordinary, hard working citizens feel a deep sense of injustice. The first is "the special case" whereby workers in certain industries or who provide particular public services are given special consideration. And who would begrudge hospital doctors, nurses, police and members of the armed forces getting special consideration for the onerous duties they perform? But of course it isn't these people at all who are treated as special cases — it is those who are militant enough to withdraw their labour, or threaten to, pending satisfaction and I must make it quite clear that the police forces, I feel, have had a raw deal for years.

And the other aspect of Government pay policy? This is the much vaunted "productivity deal". Details of such deals are usually not disclosed. Indeed when drafting this chapter there were none readily available and I commit things to memory as well as filing cabinet! Perhaps that is why there is such an over-riding feeling among those to whom I have spoken that the wool is being pulled over people's eyes. Theoretically, unions negotiate agreements whereby in return for greater output the employer makes greater reparation to his workforce and indeed I understand that the National Coal Board's productivity scheme, even though rejected out of hand by some elements of the National Union of Mineworkers initially, is now working to the mutual advantage of men and management. But until full details of all productivity deals are made public, and made challengeable, then I remain sceptical.

If the foregoing suggests that I am against trade union-
ism in any form may I state categorically that I feel trade
unions have an important role to play in industry and
commerce provided they are willing, or can be told, to act
in a reasonable way? This, however, is manifestly not the
case at present. Indeed it appears that some trade unions,
controlled by Communists and militants, believe that
they are exempt from the provisions of the law. The extent to which our Governments have been manipulated in
recent years by left wing elements and by the militants in
some unions is quite astonishing and the power of the latter must be curbed. They are a threat to every man,
woman and child and to every industrial and commercial
undertaking in this country.

Equally, it is crystal clear to me, and it must be to many
other employers, that the Government of the day cannot
be allowed to impose arbitrary sanctions against employers without making union elements equally accountable.
In other words, if a Socialist Government contrives at a
special relationship with union elements then the facts
must be readily available, before, during, or after the performance of any social contract, to enable the rest of the
nation's workforce to judge for itself whether or not such
agreements are in the best interests of the country as a
whole.

Now, to the main purpo e of this contribution — to outline the Labour Party's plans for the UK construction
industry and how, through the principal contracting fed-
erations — the National Federation of Building Trades
Employers, and the Federation of Civil Engineering Con-
tractors — we have fought, and continue to fight this
menace.

In order to understand why I, as the Founder and
Managing Director of the Taylor Woodrow Group,
regard these odious proposals as nothing less than theft
perhaps I could give a brief resume of my company's his-

tory. In 1921, as a young man of 16, I set about building two semi-detached houses in Blackpool — they still stand incidentally — and though I had intended them to be occupied by my family and by relatives, people made offers that I could not refuse and so I sold them. Many houses later my patient family were re-housed and my little business was prospering. Today, the splendid team of people which make up the Taylor Woodrow Group are actively engaged in projects of great scope and enormous diversity around the world.

But of course a great deal has happened in the interim and though there have been many important milestones in the Taylor Woodrow story — the world's first nuclear power station for example at Calder Hall, the many major projects we were involved in to assist the war effort, the expansion of our overseas operations — there was one milestone of over-riding importance and that was the decision to move south in the early thirties. By good fortune, I had heard that AEC, a privately-owned firm which made buses and lorries, was moving its operation to Southall in West London and that there would be a need for hundreds of houses to accommodate the workforce. Without delay, I travelled to London and discovered that the nearest available piece of land, some 120 acres of farmland, had been rejected by both farmers and developers for the simple reason that it sloped the wrong way and was therefore deemed to be undrainable. But it wasn't of course, not if you were prepared to go to the trouble of installing a pumping station, which we did, and soon the construction of those 1,200 houses at Grange Park, Hayes was underway. The job took us three and a half years altogether and could not have been achieved without the manager of the local Midland Bank's faith in our scheme and his faith in free enterprise. Today, it will probably come as no surprise to learn that the Group's main account is still held by the Midland Bank — at that same local branch.

The reason that I mention this incident is because in the period between AEC has been swallowed up by British Leyland — or BL as it prefers to be known — and as I write I learn that Southall's largest employer, AEC, faces total shutdown with the loss of 2,150 jobs. That is a poignant demonstration of how thriving, prosperous, private companies which have been absorbed by the State can meet an early, entirely unnecessary demise in my view. This company, which has achieved a certain immortality for its famous red London buses, quite apart from its other products, would appear to have been discriminated against by its management, and indirectly the Government, since everyone knows that the real industrial problems with BL have centred on the Midlands.

But back to the Labour Party threat. At the Party's conference in Blackpool in 1977 delegates unanimously adopted a document which they had not even seen; worse, they were swayed by an abstract in the Labour Party's National Executive Committee's conference blurb and an impassioned speech by carpenter-turned-Parliamentarian, Eric Heffer, Labour MP for Walton, Liverpool who is sponsored by UCATT (the Union of Construction Allied Trades and Technicians).

In that speech Mr. Heffer made it quite clear that his ultimate object was the nationalisation of the UK private sector building and civil engineering industries without actually saying so. He said: "We also believe that we need to extend public ownership (in the industry) on a wider basis. We are calling for the establishment of a National Construction Corporation and we believe that the basis of that National Construction Corporation must be the taking over of one or two major companies and we can build up from there. We believe that we ought to argue for public ownership in the industry, *step by step*, because it is the only sure answer to solving the difficult problems that we have".

Publication of the eventual document — commonly

referred to as "the little brown book" and entitled "Building Britain's Future: Labour's Policy on Construction" — ensued and that was the signal for the UK building and civil engineering industries to unite, and condemn with one voice, the proposals contained therein. That battle has been going on ever since and I am confident that we shall continue to fight until this threat is lifted. The Chairman of the Campaign Against Building Industry Nationalisation, Sir Maurice Laing, has affirmed that the fight goes on and the Taylor Woodrow team supports him and CABIN entirely.

Meanwhile, Eric Heffer has witnessed the depth of feeling within our industries and for some months has been at great pains to state that it is all a misunderstanding. CABIN is over-reacting and there is no threat of a State takeover; better to spend their money on positive benefits for their workforces, he says, than on balloons and bunting, posters and pamphlets, rallies and rhetoric. Well, having seen what has happened to British Shipbuilders and British Steel, British Leyland and British Rail, and the host of other publicly-owned, politically manipulated industries we are determined to fight and *ensure that it shall not happen to us*!!

Some comments on Choice
from *Bachman's Book of Freedom Quotations*

LUDWIG von MISES
The consumer is according to legend simply defenceless against high pressure advertising. If this were true, success or failure in business would depend upon the mode of advertising only. However nobody believes that any kind of advertising would have succeeded in making candle makers hold the field against the electric bulb.
(*Human Action*)

The owners of the material factors of production and the entrepreneurs are virtually mandatories or trustees of the consumers, revocably appointed by an election daily repeated.
(*Human Action*)

RABBI NACHMAN
The world was created only for the sake of the choice and choosing one.
(*Sayings or Rabbi Nachman, from The Tales of Rabbi Nachman, by Martin Buber*)

PRINCE PHILIP
Without diversity there would be no choice and without choice there is no freedom.
(*A Place for the Individual — Royal Society of Arts Lecture, 1976*)

SENECA, BISHOP OF PICENUM
. . . that man can achieve happiness by his free choice, supported by the goodness of human nature.

WILLIAM SHAKESPEARE
Thou hast power to choose.
(*All's Well That Ends Well*)

MARGARET THATCHER
My real reason for believing in the future of Britain and America is because freedom under the law, the essence of our constitutions — is something that both honours human dignity and at the same time provides the economic opportunity to bring greater prosperity to our people — a personal prosperity based on individual choice.
(*National Press Club, Washington, 1975*)

Teresa Gorman is founder and General Secretary of ASP, the Alliance of Small Firms and Self Employed People.

Her career has been divided into roughly two equal parts the first as a teacher, the second in business. She is the founder of a small company which designs and makes teaching aids.

Daughter of a self-employed demolition worker she left school at fifteen and tried a variety of jobs before deciding to teach. She then acquired various academic qualifications needed for the job.

However, like most proprietors of small firms, she has no formal business qualifications.

8

THE MANIA FOR CREDENTIALS — A THREAT TO SMALL FIRMS
by Teresa Gorman

Most people know that businesses are started by individuals, what is less well known is that, with the exception of the professions, most of these individuals have, to quote Samuel Smiles "come up from the ranks". They are predominantly from the skilled working class, with little or no formal education beyond the statutory school leaving age and no formal qualifications for their work. Some may not have had the opportunity to stay on at school but for the majority formal schooling has little interest. They belong to that small but vital group of people whose school reports, like those of Winston Churchill and Albert Einstein, predict disaster for them in adult life.

Others, start their businesses some time after leaving school and in a field where they have little or no previous experience, they learn what they need from books, as did Bernard and Laura Ashley, whose company Laura Ashley is now enjoying world wide success. One thing is certain; if these businessmen were required by law to obtain formal qualifications for their jobs many of them would not be in business at all.

The open society where such talent flourishes is now seriously threatened by the growing mania for credentials. Vested interests in the government, education, trade unions, trade associations and now the EEC are pressing for regulation and control. Not only are standard qualifications envisaged for every type of job but existing businesses are to be registered and new ones forced to apply for a licence to trade. Even the materials with which people work are subject to more and more controls with severe penalties for using those which have not been approved by some government appointed body. Not since the trade and merchant guilds of the Middle Ages exercised their suffocating grip, has society faced such a threat.

Case histories

A study of the early lives of the people who start new firms shows a number of other common elements. They try out several occupations. They frequently work for small firms or in a family business where they get the chance to see the complete pattern of an enterprise. And there is often an element of hardship such as the loss of a job or some other form of rejection. This combination seems to be a vital chemistry, as vital to their development as the detailed and formal training necessary for, say, an airline pilot. This background is shared by local tradesmen who service our daily needs and those who become the giants of industrial development. Men like Richard Arkwright, William Morris and Andrew Carnegie, all of whom, received the barest of elementary educations and went on to introduce mass production techniques into the manufacture of cotton, motor cars and steel. They improved the quality of life for the masses to a degree which few "educated" people have done. William Morris, (Lord Nuffield) and Andrew Carnegie founded charitable trusts which made them amongst the greatest of public benefactors ever known as many an academic in search of a research grant has reason to know. Carnegie donated over $350 billion dollars to charity in his lifetime and founded the United States public library service. The men who founded Marks & Spencer,

Sainsburys, Unilever, Taylor-Woodrow all began in a similar way.

Knowing the pattern it might be sensible to copy it if we want to encourage new enterprises but the opposite is happening. If these men were in school today everything would be done to steer them through formal educational channels into the ranks of the white-collared middle class.

Formal education deters enterprise

The middle classes place a high priority on security and see higher education as the route to it so it is not surprising that they are a poor source of new firms.

Empirical evidence suggests that higher education actually deters people from starting a business of their own. It is easy to see why. Academic credentials are the passport to a secure job in an established organisation where an important element in progress is the length of service. To break out of this hierarchical structure, risking seniority and pension rights for the chance of being your own boss, takes a strong nerve or a very strong stimulus.

On the other hand, people with only a basic education are more likely to work in small firms where the boss is likely to be self-taught and is much less interested in academic qualifications. He may even be suspicious of them. But work here is less secure and the opportunities for promotion are fewer. For these employees starting a business of their own may represent not only independence but a kind of security as well. There should be plenty of room for these contrasting patterns to co-exist but unfortunately the people with credentials dominate politically influential institutions, not least Parliament itself and they continually seek to impose their formal standards on the informal, small firms, sector.

Henry Ford, founder of the Ford Motor Company,

once said that he never read books because they "mussed up his mind". It is arguable that for many youngsters the best education they could get is not in the formal atmosphere of school but in the world of work, perhaps riding as passengers in the cab of a lorry, learning geography, road sense and customer relations whilst helping the owner-driver with his job. Who knows what future improvements in our transport system might come from such an education? But amongst those who do their best to prevent it are the education authorities, the wages inspectorate who enforce unrealistic minimum wages, the health and safety inspector and the EEC which has introduced the tachograph or "spy in the cab". This instrument, the ultimate in snooping, effectively prevents overtime and therefore the chance to build up the capital necessary to get a lorry of one's own. (It also forces the driver to break up his journeys into inappropriate lengths when, for the sake of another hour's driving he could be tucked up at home in bed.) These are by no means all the ways in which the independent haulier is threatened by bureaucracy but they will do to illustrate the unnecessary obstacles placed in his path.

Thus do the middle classes impress their inappropriate attitudes and values on the rest of society to the detriment of new enterprises.

The danger to immigrant enterprises

The enterprises of immigrants play a crucial part in the success of Western economy. The rapid progress of America in the nineteenth century owes more to the immigrant nature of its population than to their intellectual capabilities. The Diaspora has played a greater role in the success of Jewish enterprises than a surfeit of natural talent. Untutored Irish entrepreneurs played a key role in building our modern road, railway and underground systems.

More recently, rundown shopping areas in our cities

have been re-vitalised by Indian, Cypriot and Chinese businessmen many of whom can hardly speak our language but yet make a living, a profit, and create employment in areas where the native proprietors have given up. Britain's garment industry from which the country derives a great deal of prestige, is largely owned and staffed by first or second generation immigrants. So, too, is the mainstay of our tourist trade, the hotel and catering industry. A significant number of the people whose enterprise has earned them a place in the annual honours list have come to this country as untutored immigrants. How would these people have fared if they had had to pass a language test in order to acquire the necessary certification on which the granting of a licence would depend?

Developing patterns of discouragement

The Treaty of Rome called for the development of a *uniform* market to facilitate trade; in the hands of Brussels this becomes a command to *standardise* everything. It is hard to see how even the resilience of the free enterprise system will be able to resist the onslaught of the Brussels bureaucracy. In 1977 alone the EEC turned out directives equivalent to the contents of twenty London telephone directories; regulations affecting the minutia of daily commercial and industrial life, from the size of cauliflowers to the detailed components of motor vehicles. It hardly needs to be said that rules of this kind will fossilise agricultural as well as industrial and commercial practices because innovation, by definition, defies existing rules.

At home since World War II fifty-five thousand pages of new laws have been passed by Parliament. These have created a large number of quasi-autonomous non governmental organisations (Quangos), with statutory powers to introduce new regulations which do not even need parliamentary approval.

The joint industrial boards which have been appointed

to oversee those industries not already nationalised, exercise control through so-called voluntary registers. An example is the demolition register operating in the building and construction industry. Private demolition companies are invited to join. One of the inducements is that local and central government demolition work is restricted to firms who have registered. These firms must agree to deal only with other approved firms if they are sub-contracting their work and they must agree to use only trade union labour. And so a stockade is erected against those who refuse to conform.

Certification poses problems not only for people who may wish to change jobs but to people whose talents do not run along academic lines. One peculiar variety of certification with particularly sinister overtones is the introduction of the Tax Exemption Certificate for sub-contractors in the building and construction industry. Rules for obtaining these certificates are laid down by the Inland Revenue who used them to exclude over 45,000 applicants when the scheme was introduced in 1976. Technically a sub-contractor can continue to work without the certificate but it is made much more difficult for him. A large part of his gross earnings must be retained by the contractor and sent to the Inland Revenue. This plays havoc with the cash flow of a small firm in an industry where work is spasmodic. Tax collectors, to whom efficient book-keeping is more important than the ability to lay bricks, now effectively control a large part of the labour force of the building and construction industry.

Licensing is the ultimate stage of control. To carry on a licensed trade without permission is a punishable offence. One by one the openings for self-employment are being regulated in this way from mini-cabbing to baby-minding. It is not hard to see that young people, and especially those who have been unable to negotiate the hurdles of formal school examinations, will gradually be prevented from setting up in business.

Possibility of change

The steam roller of regulation is on a downward slope and threatens those enterprising individuals whose rare but largely untutored talents are far more precious than the ability to conform. Parliament is heavily loaded with representatives from the society of credential holders, with teachers, lawyers and other professionals predominating. They are easy meat for pressure groups who see legislation as a way to iron out society's little wrinkles.

The media, also replete with the products of higher education, favour, with rare exceptions, the formalisation of society. Thus, reports from the Office of Fair Trading, receive extensive news coverage rarely balanced by the opinions of those most harmed by their activities.

Schools teach the standard anti-capitalist version of history with all the myths of the evils of the Industrial Revolution; a revolution which gave working class people their first real chance of upward mobility. Yet in spite of the puritanical onslaught against material success to which they are subjected in the class-room and from the media, young people still look up to those of their contemporaries who have achieved it, albeit mainly pop stars, television personalities and sports heroes.

If the works of Samuel Smiles and Adam Smith were taught in schools instead of those of Charles Dickens and Karl Marx, it would do much to foster this latent self-interest and encourage them to look around for opportunities of setting up in businesses of their own. And what a relief it would be for them to know that to be a Freddie Laker or a Mary Quant it is not necessary to jump the educational hurdles which lead to the sixth-form.

If we are to keep open these traditional avenues to new enterprise we must rigorously reject schemes, however plausible, to raise standards by regulation and wage war on the statutes which already threaten the open society.

Dennis Greig, who is the grandson of famous provision merchant David Greig, went to New College, Oxford in 1938 but left after only one year because of the war. He joined the Royal Air Force but was invalided out in 1945 and began farming near Dover. On the death of his grandfather in 1952 he joined his father, Ross Greig, and his brother in London in the family business. He maintained his farming interests on his own farm at Four Elms and in his spare time built up one of the first broiler chicken groups, eventually producing 50,000 chickens per week and packing 60,000 *dozen* eggs weekly for the retail trade. After the sale of David Greig Limited in 1973 he concentrated on farming with an interest in a few small private enterprise businesses.

He is married with five children and two grandchildren. His eldest son works in the Dewhurst meat retail chain, one is at Wye Agricultural College, the youngest at public school, while his daughters are in Hong Kong.

Dennis Greig has been active in the Leonard Cheshire Homes since 1966, became chairman of Seven Springs at Tunbridge Wells and is now a Trustee of the Cheshire Foundation.

He says he has a "wonderful wife who does much more than I do — and a young mother of 86 who keeps me and the family up to standard!"

9

SERVING THE CUSTOMER
WELL
by Dennis Greig

It is remarkable that private enterprise and small businesses still survive in the United Kingdom when our modern society seems largely dedicated to the elimination of both.

But, praise be, there are still those who are ready to risk much and push themselves beyond the bounds of normal effort to create and foster new private enterprises. Over the centuries, in all parts of the world, there have at different times been eras of private endeavour as opposed to State monopoly. Today there are still large areas where private enterprise remains dominant, although mostly alongside considerable — and increasing — state and nationalised industry. On the other hand there are also numerous examples of total state monopoly, notably in the USSR where economic successes are insignificant despite military power and leadership in space research. Where the private citizen is concerned and the living standards of the people generally are taken into account then the comparison with the largely private enterprise system of the West shows the enormous advantages of living in the countries of Western Europe or in North America.

This is not to infer that all private enterprise is successful or that every person as of right enjoys a higher standard of living in a private enterprise system, but there seems ample evidence that private enterprise benefits the consumer directly and contributes to government revenue while exercising a positive effect on nationalised industries through competitive performance.

Despite everything the Private Sector in this country continues to be active and every day witnesses new examples of individual enterprise. It is perhaps the challenge to human pride and confidence or the "fire in the belly" but perhaps most of all it is hunger after personal rewards. My great grandmother, over one hundred years ago, having a large family to care for on comparatively meagre resources, enterprisingly turned her hand to doing what she knew best, namely preparing food to sell. "What I cannot sell, my children can eat" and who would know better than the mother of a large family what her customers really wanted.

From such a humble beginning grew a great family food business, but not without hard work and considerable risks. "Nothing without labour" was the favourite motto of her eldest son. Even before leaving school, he was helping in the little business begun by his mother in her kitchen. On leaving school he was apprenticed to a large successful foodstore to widen his own knowledge and then at a very early age David Greig launched out on his own.

This meant in practice living over the shop, the better to work the long hours demanded and to keep a constant watch on all that had to be done. Right from the start he began to develop a personal link with his customers, a vital bond which can often guarantee satisfaction and success for both.

The business prospered well with more retail shops being opened in a closely knit area, the young entrepreneur using a bicycle in order to maintain frequent contact with his outlets. The hours of work, even by the standards of those far-off days, were long and arduous, but the rewards were there to be won by providing customers with the foods they wanted at prices they could afford.

The owner gathered about himself others of like ideals, fashioned in his own mould, in order to widen the circle in a similar pattern. All the staff members could feel themselves to be part of a dynamic unit dedicated to serve the customer. It is noteworthy that on the founder's death at 86 some of the staff from the early days had still been working with the "old Guvnor". Many people gave a lifetime's service to that one family business. Such links are forged fine and strong.

Similar links were established between the business and its suppliers as well as with its customers. For example, as trade grew there sprang up direct contacts with suppliers of Dutch butter, Italian cheese, Danish bacon, and eggs from Russia and Poland. My own Godfather was that same Italian cheese supplier, while the Russian egg merchant eventually had to flee his country from the Bolsheviks. He started an egg packing business in Denmark for my Grandfather and this lasted until the last war when the Germans marched in. Evening calls by telephone to the butter merchant in Holland were commonplace in our household. Such a business meant an intensely personal interest for all connected with it. The maintenance of standards of quality was paramount, and the fierceness of competition ensured the keenest value for the customer.

Indeed, the High Street war in those days was as sharp as ever it is now, albeit on a rather less flamboyant scale. It was normal for foodshops to be close together so that in order to capture and satisfy the local demand the retailer had to pay constant attention to every detail of his trade, for customers had literally only to walk a few yards looking into foodshop windows to compare prices and quality.

Now as then it is in fact the intense competition between various private traders which ensures maximum value for their customers. But if *prices* can be easily compared, how can the customer feel assured of high *quality* and good *value*? Here the reputation of the private trader or family trader is of paramount importance. It is extremely close contact with the consumer which still counts for so much.

To illustrate this, I recall that in our family business we actually produced many items ourselves — as had Great Grandmother many decades earlier — cakes, sausages, pies etc. Prior to the last war, our cake bakery had established a reputation for the use of "genuine" ingredients, such as butter and *shell eggs*, but this was impossible during wartime. However, as soon as post-war conditions allowed it was a joy for the bakery manager to revert to such practices which involved, among other operations, the cracking of thousands of fresh eggs daily. It was a means of giving a small business the edge on the bigger firms by doing something just a bit better with the result that customers showed their appreciation in no uncertain way. It had the effect of upgrading the whole market, not only for one particular product or in one separate outlet but generally throughout the trade. Undoubtedly this healthy competition as much as the determination of the trader to capture his share of the market by pleasing consumers, however small that trader might be, ensured continuing standards of quality and value, a state of affairs that would soon disappear in a society devoid of private traders eager to establish their presence.

As trade and fashions change, as they must, in every business there should still be the same spirit of giving good service. In many ways self-service has meant a drift away from the personal service described above. This in itself provides a challenge to the smaller businessman to attend to customers' requirements more closely. In fact the trend towards "Big is Beautiful" leaves behind it a vacuum which will no doubt always be filled by the small man for as long as Private Enterprise is allowed to exist. Recently I was able to encourage two young men to set up on their own in the tea trade, supposedly dominated by the giants, and the "crumbs" they are gathering are a credit to their endeavours to ensure a more personalised service to their customers.

It may seem a long way — indeed it is a long time, over a century ago — from a resourceful woman's own efforts at her kitchen table to supply needs beyond her own family — but the small businessman who is the heart and soul of much Private Enterprise, will always be doing just what he may feel suits him and fulfils a consumer need.

Ralph Harris was born in 1924 and educated at Tottenham Grammar School and Queens' College, Cambridge. He was Lecturer in Political Economy at St. Andrews University, 1949-56, and has been General Director of the Institute of Economic Affairs since 1957. He wrote (with Arthur Seldon), *Hire Purchase in a Free Society, Advertising in a Free Society, Choice in Welfare*, etc., for the IEA. His essay, 'In Place of Incomes Policy', was published in *Catch '76. . .?* (Occasional Paper 'Special' (No. 47), 1976). A more recent work, written with Arthur Seldon, is *Pricing or Taxing* (Hobart Paper No. 71). He is Secretary of the Wincott Foundation and the Political Economy Club, formerly secretary, now a Vice-President, of the Mont Pelerin Society, and a Council Member of University College, Buckingham. Mr Harris lectures and writes widely on post-war policies and economic requirements of free society.

10

THE FREE MARKET
THE CHALLENGE TO COLLECTIVISM
by Ralph Harris

Most major disagreements about economic policy can for practical purposes be represented as a tug-of-war between two views of the ability of politicians to promote economic welfare. The classical liberal conception saw an essential but limited role for government to enforce a framework of laws and institutions that would advance economic freedom and prosperity by the fertile interplay of competitive enterprise with consumer choice. The opposite, collectivist, conception saw almost unlimited scope for government to improve social welfare by restricting the freedom of individuals as producers, traders, property-owners and consumers.

The striking discrepancy between the good intentions of politicians and their poor performance illustrates a fundamental difference in analysis between the contrasting approaches and expectations of the classical and collectivist schools of thought. All economists start from the scarcity of human and material resources in relation to the demands upon them. The moment we turn to the choice between alternative ways of using scarce resources most effectively to yield the maximum output of (valued) goods and services, their paths diverge sharply. The core of the collectivist faith is that the "public interest" in production and consumption can be identified and imposed directly by governments taking power to over-ride the judgement of individuals informed by their personal preferences and interests. The instant appeal to both heart and mind of this general proposition is sufficiently strong to withstand a good deal of contact with disappointing reality.

The classical view, which has much less immediate or emotional appeal, sees the public interest emerging spontaneously as a by-product of individuals more or less freely pursuing their own interests. When critics warn against the appeal to self-interest as pandering to "greed", "profiteering", "selfishness", they are unwittingly paying eloquent tribute to the strength of the motive power which Adam Smith described more dispassionately as "the effort of every man to better his condition". Platform rhetoric aside, honest introspection no less than observation will certainly confirm that people work more conscientiously and consistently when there is something at stake in the outcome for themselves, their families, or indeed for any interest they can easily identify with their own, including unselfish causes and charity. There is little room for disagreement about the force and tenacity of "self-interest" in this sense. The difference is that the collectivist sees it as generally in conflict with what he regards as the "public interest", whilst the liberal believes the two can be reconciled with the minimum of detailed interference by government.

Without undue violence to the profound philosophical issues, the key question can be put in more homely terms. Since we each see our personal interest more clearly and consistently than that of our neighbours, how can we best be prevented from pursuing it at their expense? The answer of the classical liberal economist is that the most effective — indeed the only dependable — check to the abuse of self-interest is nothing more nor less than a competitive market. At its simplest, every producer is disciplined by the prospect of losing sales if he pushes his price above that which others are content to ask for a similar product or service.

Motives versus outcome

It is from this central commonsense proposition that economists in the classical tradition have elaborated and refined a technique of market analysis which, we believe, provides a more serviceable guide for policy than the question-begging assertions about "the public interest" on which the collectivist consensus has relied since the war. If sceptics are to give a fair hearing to the argument that follows, however, an essential pre-condition is to be on guard against the widespread confusion between *motives* and *outcome*. It is easy to demonstrate from post-war experience that the most single-minded, even high-minded, dedication to the "public interest" provides no guarantee of success. It is more difficult for the layman to grasp that by allowing people generally to act in the light of their own interests, which includes "selflessness" in pursuing self-chosen *unselfish* causes, something more recognisable as the true public interest may emerge. Thus so long as competition between suppliers prevails in the market, they can advance their chosen interests only by serving that of the consumer. Adam Smith's famous quotation is worth pondering afresh:

> "It is not from the benevolence of the butcher, the brewer, or the baker that we expect our dinner, but from their regard to their own interest."

Likewise, when the investor (or worker) is considering how best to employ his capital (or labour), Smith assumes "it is his own advantage and not that of society which he has in view" but, he continues in one of the most celebrated passages from *The Wealth of Nations*:

> "... he is in this as in many other cases led by an invisible hand to promote an end which was no part of his intention. By pursuing his own interest he frequently promotes that of society more effectually than when he really intends to promote it. I have never known much good done by those who affected

to trade in the public interest."

The market does not assume men are omniscient saints; it takes them as they are and transmutes parochial concerns into public good.

Need for competition

From this underlying postulate that competitive markets can bring harmony between the private and public interests, far-reaching implications can be derived. The first is that both buyers and sellers must gain from trading on price and other terms which they freely choose to accept. The prevalence of competition reconciles what might otherwise be the opposing interests of suppliers (in high prices) and consumers (in low prices) by creating a common interest in doing business at the ruling market price. The competitive process is not, in the jargon, a "zero-sum game" in which some gain only at the expense of others. It is a social mechanism that converts potentially conflicting interests into "mutual gains from trade".

A second implication is that changes in the supply of or demand for a product can be brought into balance by the impersonal mechanism of an increase or reduction in price. Changes in price act as signals to producers and consumers to co-operate without collusion in restoring an approximate balance (if not the textbook "equilibrium") which was disturbed by shifts in demand or supply. The "imperfections" of the market — through inequality of incomes, monopoly, "externalities" — do not make it inferior to the alternative of government which in practice has its own imperfections that are more difficult to correct, not least because escape from unacceptable (public) suppliers is difficult or impossible.

Above all, competition prevents the abuse of powerful producer interests by giving the consumer the final say in determining their fortunes. When we talk of "the sovereignty of the consumer", we mean nothing less than that only so long as there is competition among suppliers can the generality of buyers decide which of them will prosper. Markets offer "exits" that make consumer "voices" effective. There may be delays, as for example when a declining firm increases advertising to try and restore demand, but in the end no business can flourish unless it gives good value to its customers and is responsive to their changing preferences.

Although it follows that the consumers' interest — whether in cheapness, quality, service or other features — is not in conflict with a (successful) firm's interest in selling its products, it remains true that any supplier would stand to gain from a restriction of competition that enabled him to raise his price (or lower quality, etc.) without losing sales. But when competition is infringed by a dominant or monopoly supplier, the harmony with consumers in that market is replaced by what may properly be called "exploitation": the imposition of a price higher than the minimum which an efficient producer would charge in competitive conditions.

The universal consumer interest

Thus the harmony Smith likened to the product of "an invisible hand" is in practice the result of competition which compels the producer to give satisfaction to his customers. And since, as Smith also postulated, "Consumption is the sole end and purpose of all production", it is the universal, common consumer interest which should prevail against the particular, partial, producer interest. This principle of harmony can be expressed with even wider generality. So far we have sketched the way competition reconciles the apparently conflicting interests of buyers and sellers in markets for products which determine the profits of enterprises. But much the same analysis holds good in principle for markets in labour, saving and land which give rise to factor prices in the form of wages (and salaries), interest and rent. In all cases, competition among suppliers is necessary to uphold the universal consumer interest against "exploitation".

A deduction is that government should, *with the minimum of exceptions*, confine access to income by all participants in economic activity to the profits, wages, interest and rent that can be earned from competitive markets in which the general community of consumers rule the roost. There will, of course, be familiar social welfare grounds for conferring "public income" on the old, handicapped and others not capable of earning an adequate income from competitive economic activity. But unless such exceptions are narrowly defined — which does not mean treated ungenerously — the door will be opened to a fragmentation of the market order and a disruption of the general harmony it is capable of providing.

Consider a producer (or union) that is dissatisfied with the profit (or wage) its investors (or employees) can earn in the market in which its capital (or labour) is employed. A familiar resort is for its spokesmen to appeal to government for protection against imports or for other checks on competition that would enable its members to escape from consumer sovereignty and extort a higher income by raising prices. Once government has yielded to such a pressure group, a conflict between sectional private interests and the general interest is opened up and there will be a queue of other "special cases" ready to plead with equal plausibility for exemptions from the discipline of competition.

Some contest the sovereignty of the consumer on the ground that consumers are also producers and that the impact of changes in techniques or markets may impose painful adjustments on suppliers or workers whose products or jobs are threatened with decline. The classical retort is that the costs of such continuous adjustments by producers are worth paying to preserve the wider consumer benefits from competition. On this reckoning, the best way of easing change is, firstly, by some form of minimum income support, and, secondly, by encouraging mobility of labour and other factors to move into alternative lines of production with better prospects. The market does not offer lives of comfort from disturbance, but it makes the impact of unavoidable change gradual in contrast to the protectionist alternatives — from the guild system through syndicalism to communism — in which change eventually forces its way by commotion, convulsion and violence.

Beggar-my-neighbour

If the interplay of consumer choice and producer competition acts like the philosopher's stone to transmute "self-interest" into the general interest, a reverse alchemy comes into play when politicians try to impede this process. However good their motives to help particular groups, they invariably end up impoverishing even the intended beneficiaries. Thus the further law departs from general rules to facilitate competition, and lapses into favouring or frustrating particular activities, the more it erodes both efficiency and freedom. The alternative to Smith's "invisible hand" becomes the state's "visible fist", since government interference requires the increasing use of coercion — whether by discriminatory taxes and subsidies or by outright prohibition.*

Economists of the classical tradition are falsely accused of ideology in resisting exceptions to the rules of competition. Yet their concern can be upheld on the twin pillars of equity and efficiency. Once governments start

* If a number of special concessions are made, the liberal economist prefers government intervention to take the form of open taxes or subsidies which at least indicate the cost of protectionism, rather than prohibitions which conceal the extent of distortion.

down the road of protecting sectional interests by restricting competition, there is no natural halting place short of generalised restrictionism. The dilemma is that if favours are given to one group, it is a logical deployment of self interest for others to seek similar, or larger, favours. The wider any privilege is extended, the more it is attenuated and the less benefit it confers on each recipient. In economic analysis, to suppose all can gain from the spread of beggar-my-neighbour policies is to fall into the crudest fallacy of composition. Can there by any doubt that in Britain we have long passed the point where all or most are losing — no doubt unequally and inequitably — from the use of the political process by all or most in an effort to enrich ourselves at the expense of all or most? This is indeed the war of all against all.

Once the presumption in favour of consumer sovereignty and competitive markets is undermined by dispensations to sectional interests, political cohesion itself is imperilled. As Professor F.A. Hayek has shown,* government in western democracies is highly vulnerable to pressures from organised groups offering electoral (and financial) support in return for privileges. The wider this process spreads, the more governments become coalitions of organised interests, and the more hostages they offer to producers at the expense of the common interest of consumers. The result is not only a weakening of the efficiency and adaptation of production to changing conditions; it is also a spreading disillusion as each favoured group finds its anticipated advantages cancelled out by the proliferation of favours all round. This source of mistrust and even contempt for politicians is none the less real for being generally not understood. Unlimited government thus leads inexorably to unlimited disenchant-

* *Economic Freedom and Representative Government*, Occasional Paper 39, 1973 (2nd impression 1976).

ment.§ And the pace of collectivism accelerates, not because that is what people want but as the unintended outcome of diverse, conflicting but cumulative demands for favoured treatment.

It is the most naive error to suppose that the main conflict of interest is between "capital" and "labour". If one trade union can impose higher wages by restriction of entry, the cost is not borne by investors, who can escape, but by other workers who could do the job but are excluded, and by the consumers who pay higher prices for the product. But as union restrictionism spreads, the expected producers' gains are lost in generally higher consumer prices. Thus the benefit of monopoly (for wages or profits) depends on a differential advantage which vanishes when others join in the same game.

The spread of protectionism

It is not fanciful to chart the long decline in Britain's economic performance against the fall from favour of the broad classical liberal precepts for economic policy. Britain had become the workshop and banker of the world at a time when economic liberalism was at its height. Only around the end of the 19th century when our industrial predominance was challenged by European and American competition did political discussion return to the possibility of tariff protection — in the supposed interests of wages and employment as well as of profits and capital. The plain choice was between embracing the risks and opportunities of adapting to new markets or resisting change in defence of the vested interests.

This is the conflict at the heart of British economic and social policy which dates back at least to the beginning of the century. It is succinctly summed up in *The Clash of*

§ Hayek's solution is by constitutional reform to limit the power of the elected majority to concede favours to powerful importunity.

Progress and Security, the title of a neglected volume written by Professor A.G.B. Fisher in 1935.* The central argument, based on *a priori* liberal analysis and confirmed by historical observation, is that a progressive economy must be characterised by change and uncertainty caused by the impact of new techniques, products, resources, demands. The rate of advance in standards of living therefore depends on the ease with which labour and other factors of production can be transferred from declining firms and industries where their value is falling into expanding markets where their value is rising. The dilemma for economic and social policy is that, whilst everyone wants the fruits of material progress — in leisure or other amenities if not in more consumption — as workers and capitalists they naturally resist the disturbance to their present employment and investment without which material progress is frustrated.

Even before 1914, a powerful wing of the Conservative Party was campaigning to reverse the classic doctrine of free trade in the name of Imperial preference. Simultaneously, the new Labour Party was emerging as the avowed political arm of the trade unions and in 1906 had persuaded a nominally Liberal Government to confer on those embryonic labour monopolies what Dicey declared to be "privilege and protection not possessed by any other person or body of persons."§

The 1914-18 war gave a massive impetus to the forces making for protectionism. Thereafter, the post-war slump — deepened by the inept return to the gold standard at an over-valued parity — provided plenty of pretexts for prolonging and even extending the damaging process. In 1931 the final departure from free trade gave

* Published by Macmillan.

§ Preface to the second edition of *Law and Opinion in England*, Macmillan, 1914.

"safety first" politicians a protected home market in which to insulate the great basic industries still further from the competitive markets under the slogan of "rationalisation". In the words of the leading authority on the structure of British industry:

> "the chief effect of government intervention between the wars was to defend the failure rather than to encourage the enterprising".*

The Labour Party that came into power in 1945 took over a mostly debilitated economy but was sustained by an unusually widespread degree of goodwill. Reacting against the memory of pre-war unemployment — but not against its true cause — the Government proclaimed its aims as full employment and the welfare state which were to be achieved by planning, with nationalisation reserved for the run-down basic industries. The danger glimpsed by liberal economists was that such an approach would reinforce most of the conservative — in the sense of conservationist — elements in public policy that had made for economic rigidity between the wars. But only the politically-jaundiced could question the high integrity and intelligence of such leading members of the Government as Attlee, Cripps, Dalton, Bevin, Bevan, Shawcross. The question was simply whether their collective good intentions would prevail against their chosen collectivist methods.

Among the foremost champions of the great classical tradition, Professor (later Sir) Dennis Robertson did not conceal his doubts. In his 1949 Presidential lecture to the Royal Economic Society, under the title "On Sticking to One's Last", he warned fellow economists against "betraying their calling" by coming to terms with "the changed temper of the age". He went on:

* Professor G.C. Allen in *The British Disease*, Hobart Paper 67, 1976.

109

"... it takes some spirit to state clearly and fairly the case for wage reduction as a cure for unemployment or an adverse balance of payments, or the case for the curtailment of subsidies and the overhauling of social services as a solvent of inflationary pressure, without being prematurely silenced by the argument that nowadays the trade unions would never stand for such things. Perhaps they wouldn't, but that is no reason for not following the argument whithersoever it leads. But it is easier flogging dead horses than taming live ones; and some of those who display great retrospective gallantry against the fallacies and obscurantisms of yesterday seem to me somewhat over-hasty to make their peace with those of today."

Similar unheeded doubts were voiced by such senior economists as Lionel (now Lord) Robbins, John Jewkes, Sir Arnold Plant, Frank Paish, James Meade, Roy Harrod. There could be little doubt, however, that the political "temper of the age" was to meet every setback to government plans with calls for still more far-reaching interventions.

By the 1950s it certainly took some spirit to discuss any aspect of policy explicitly in terms of market analysis without inviting the crushing accusation of wanting to "turn back the clock". But what if the clock were wrong? What if the scorned analysis of supply and demand embodied timeless lessons — or "laws" — for the most efficient management of scarce resources consistent with the widest freedom of choice?

With a brief interlude under Churchill's banner of "Set the People Free", post-war governments of both parties have retreated still further from the competitive market economy. By 1979 the State spends more than half the national income, employs almost one-third of the labour force, owns outright all the basic industries and tries to

110

control investment, prices and incomes throughout the dwindling market sector. The bleak results mock the boasted good intentions of their perpetrators. Put to the test, the collectivist consensus has failed. Like John Brown's body it may march a little further yet; but its obituary was pronounced in The Guardian — of all unlikely places — where Peter Jenkins sadly confessed:* "it is becoming startlingly obvious that the more liberal economies are the more successful".

The above article is based on material appearing in "Not from benevolence...." by Ralph Harris and Arthur Seldon (The Institute of Economic Affairs)

---

* In a review of *The Coming Confrontation*, Hobart Paperback No. 12, edited by Arthur Seldon and published by the Institute of Economic Affairs, 1978.